Community of Love

COMMUNITY OF LOVE

JOHN MAIN

Introduction by Laurence Freeman

A Medio Media Book
Continuum • New York

1999
The Continuum Publishing Company
370 Lexington Avenue
New York, NY 10017

Printed in the United States of America

Library of Congress Cataloging-in-Publication Data

Main, John, O.S.B.
  Community of love / John Main ; introduction by Laurence Freeman.
      p.   cm.
  ISBN 0-8264-1180-0 (pbk.)
  1. Spiritual life — Catholic Church.   I. Title.
BX2350.2.M3143 1999
248.4'82—dc21   99-13592
                                                                      CIP

Contents

How to Meditate

Sit down. Sit still and upright. Close your eyes lightly. Sit relaxed but alert. Silently, interiorly begin to say a single word. We recommend the prayer-phrase "maranatha." Recite it as four syllables of equal length. Listen to it as you say it, gently but continuously. Do not think or imagine anything – spiritual or otherwise. If thoughts and images come, these are distractions at the time of meditation, so keep returning to simply saying the word. Meditate each morning and evening for between twenty and thirty minutes.

The World Community for Christian Meditation

Meditation creates community. Since the first Christian Meditation Centre was started by John Main in 1975, a steadily growing community of Christian meditators has spread around the world. Individual meditators frequently begin to meet in small weekly groups and the network of these groups provides wider support and encouragement for those who wish to sustain their daily practice of morning and evening meditation.

The groups meet in homes, parishes schools, prisons, business, religious communities and government departments. Beginning with a short teaching on meditation, often drawn from the Community's collection of taped talks by John Main, the group then meditates together in silence for half an hour. After the talk, there is time for discussion. The groups are by nature ecumenical and practice an open-door hospitality, welcoming anyone who comes sincerely seeking silence.

A growing number of Christian Meditation Centres, some residential, others located in meditators' homes, also serve to communicate the way of silence taught in this tradition. The Centres help co-ordinate the local weekly groups and organize regular retreats, seminars and other meditation events.

The International Centre in London co-ordinates this world-wide community of meditators. A quarterly newsletter, giving spiritual teaching and reflection, is sent out from London and distributed from a number of national centers, together with local and international news of retreats and other events being held in the world-wide community. An annual John Main Seminar is held in Europe and North America on alternate years.

This Centre is funded entirely by donations and especially through a Friends of the International Centre programme.

The World Community for Christian Meditation
International Centre
23 Kensington Square
London W8 5HN
United Kingdom
Tel: 44 171 937 4679 Fax: 44 171 937 6790
E-mail: wccm@compuserve.com

Visit The World Community for Christian Meditation Web site for information, weekly mediation group reading and discussion at: **www.wccm.org**

United States: Christian Meditation Centre / 1080 West Irving Park Rd. / /Roselle, IL 60172.
Tel/Fax: 1 630 351 2613

John Main Institute / 7315 Brookville Rd. / Chevy Chase, MD 20815.
Tel: 1 301 652 8635
E-mail: wmcoerp@erols.com

Christian Meditation Centre / 1619 Wright St. / Wall, NJ 07719.
Tel: 1 732 681 6238 Fax: 1 732 280 5999
E-mail: gjryan@aol.com

The Cornerstone Centre / 1215 East Missouri Ave. / Suite A 100 / Phoenix, AZ 85014-2914.
Tel: 1 602 279 3454 Fax: 1 602 957 3467
E-mail: ecrmjr@worldnet.att.net

Introduction

In the last decade of his life John Main was increasingly thought of as a teacher of meditation. This concentration sometimes surprised those who had known him before his 'rediscovery' of that Christian tradition with which his influence on the Church and secular society of the twentieth century has become associated. He was a man of many gifts and several careers, wide-ranging interests and complementary sympathies. A deeply spiritual man, a theorist, a humorist, a prophet.

Once he said that everyone has just one thing to say or to do with their life. This was surprising from a man of so many parts who could leave the past and start anew so readily. His concentration on meditation reflected his finding the one thing he had particularly to say, to do. It was his destiny and good fortune, shared and still being shared with others that he did find it. The rich variety of his life and personality thus became not a dispersal of energy but a gathering of forces that were unified in a point of intense certainty and magnanimity.

Narrow as is the path, the path that leads to life in general and the path of meditation in particular, it is not narrow-minded. The narrowness signifies a focusing not a blinkering of vision, attention not exclusion and integration rather than repression. This volume brings together John Main's thought on a wide range of subjects not specifically on the teaching of meditation. He has here clear, striking insights for modern people on some of the major issues that perplex our lives today. But his thought and insight derive their clarity from his centre of focus. Important to remember as we read his thought on the problems of Church and society, religion and death, religious and secular lifestyles, is that his focus is not theoretical or ideological, but experiental. His insights originate in experience of God and point towards the same experience for ourselves.

They are useful insights to ponder for anyone concerned for themselves, their children or their contemporaries about the spiritual health of the world today, East or West. As issues they are the fundamental questions that underlie our manifold crisis. Clear thinking is necessary to cope with crisis, and clarity requires a steady focal point. For John Main the focal point of vision is the imageless, non-conceptual centredness of the whole person, body, mind and spirit, in pure prayer. Faith is the steadiness of that point. Christ is its spiritual energy. If we want to think clearly about the immediate and long-term problems of our personal and collective lives, whether our institutional crises or our fear of dying, we need to have a clear point of departure for our reflection. John Main does not give answers. He gives a sure starting point, perhaps the only sure starting point, in personal experience. The answers lie hidden perhaps under unnoticed stones, but along a path that runs straight and true, despite its many apparent twists and turns. The final answer is, of course, always 'hidden in God', beyond thought or understanding but not beyond our experience.

We have called this volume of talks and articles by the title of a collection of talks given to oblates of the monastery John Main started in Montreal. 'Community of Love' epitomizes his deepest vision of the meaning of meditation, of the Church, of human life. 'To follow the way of meditation we need others to travel with us', he says. Solitary and personally challenging as meditation is, it transforms us from isolated components of a crowd into members of a community. John Main's own experience of the failures and setbacks of leaving one community and starting another authorized him to speak with unromantic idealism of the Christian dynamic of community, always a personal dynamic of death and resurrection.

'The Church is oceanic', he says. That is, it is vast, various and it swells and falls. But he is not content with being descriptive. He offers a prescription for the problems of the Church today and he sees recovery in a return to the traditional authority accorded to personal experience as the root and nutrition of the life of faith. External authority in such a contemplative Church is then seen to reside in teachers rather than administrators. And the teachers 'must create the community that will be the basis for their ministry'. No personality cult is risked here or excessive subjectivism, because the teacher must die, many times, before the community is created.

The fear of death is one of the deepest restrictions on growth for all individuals as well as for the communities we long to belong to and yet fear to die into. John Main suggests another aspect of this now well-acknowledged fear, in the fear we have of coming close to what we love and worship. We experience fear when we realize that the 'splendour of the Lord Jesus is so terribly close to us'. Here is a deeply useful insight, born out of the experience of meditation, which reminds us that the fear of the Lord (which includes both awe and recoil) is the end of all other fears and the beginning of wisdom.

Wisdom is not cleverness but the vision of unity. John Main saw and is helping a global movement of spiritual awakening. He knew that people needed a clear teaching on how to enter and complete the contemplative experience in which this awakening occurs. It was a teaching that could not be invented: you cannot re-invent the wheel. But it needed to be rediscovered, re-appropriated and re-expressed in the language of ordinary people. The tradition of Christian meditation, long lost in books or restrictive practices, thus rose to new and fuller life.

Tradition is something alive and active, more like a chameleon than a museum-case. And so for John Main, monks are adventurers not museum-keepers or escapees from reality. The ancient Greek Orthodox Hesychastic tradition of desert monasticism, developed by the monks of Mount Athos in the fourteenth century, now reaches out into the lives of ordinary Christians, their weekly meditation groups, parishes, places of work, universities and hospitals. Symbols, including the great personal symbols of Christian devotion, are life-giving only when they have broken free from the crust of imagery with which time encases them. From the steady focal-point of his experience of meditation all these disturbing yet reassuring insights strike us with both authority and gentleness.

In the pages that follow, John Main is a trustworthy guide through some of the thickets of modern dilemmas because of his combination of authority and respect for others' freedom.

Introduction

At times he deals with sombre themes, the deeper fears of personal and social life. Yet he is always lively and full of hope. He does not offer consolation. He was never paternalistic. He was rather the heroic leader that he saw St Benedict to be. Yet you never left his presence, or put down his books, without feeling revitalized to continue the search, not merely to endure but to enjoy.

The Benedictine Priory   LAURENCE FREEMAN OSB
Montreal
July 1989

The Hunger for Prayer

Preface

Soon after we had arrived in Montreal John Main was asked to be the keynote speaker at a congress of Canadian University Chaplains held in Kingston, Ontario. These two talks which he gave there are concerned with the challenge facing the Christian proclamation of the gospel on the university campus. But the issues raised by this challenge are universal ones – the nature of a spiritual community, the relation between the personal and the absolute in the religious experience, the role of the spiritual teacher, the dynamic of commitment, community, communication. It is the way John Main explores and explains these concerns that makes these talks a statement of importance for all of us concerned with the personal pilgrimage of the spirit and its social content and consequences.

John Main had had much experience of education and its institutions, as a professor of Law at Trinity College, Dublin, and as headmaster of a Benedictine High School in Washington, DC. From this experience he had come to see the inadequacy of a merely 'quality' education and the greater need to lead, guide and inspire the young in the values of the spiritual reality. He saw that was not to be done only by introducing them to a religious tradition or several religious traditions. It required commitment to a spiritual path, to silence as the universal language of the spirit, to the discipline of spiritual discipleship. It is a hard challenge because the religion teachers, the chaplains, must be more than an academic authority and even more than a counsellor. They must be pilgrims themselves before they can be guides.

John Main's last 'teaching institution' was also a school but a 'school of the Lord's service' as St Benedict, his guide, called it. From this community, committed to the path and communicating it generously, he taught the way to the Universal Teacher, the Lord Jesus, who is himself the way, the goal and the guide.

Laurence Freeman OSB

Meditation and the Church

Until comparatively recently many church people were quite uneasy and sceptical of the religious significance of meditation in our time – as they were of the general interest in Eastern mysticism. It has taken all of us some time to realize that a great spiritual hunger has arisen in our contemporaries; also some time to realize that this hunger is genuine. Indeed, it is probably the most striking movement of the religious instinct in human beings which most of us will see in our lifetime. It has been associated, it is true, with some eccentric, faddish and even cynical personalities or organizations, but the essential authenticity of this movement is indicated by the fact that these nine-day wonders *do* die out and do not become, on the whole, fanatical. As our contemporaries search for the real religious dimension of their life they are making many mistakes, putting their faith in many false prophets, but they continue to return to the path of sincere openness which is the essential nature of their pilgrimage and of their search.

If it has taken us a long while to understand the power of this hunger of spirit it is taking us even longer to realize why these people are not, on the whole, looking to the Christian Church, at least the Church in its Western incarnation, to satisfy this hunger. To many, the Church, with all its 'church-iness' and self-conscious preoccupation with updating its own image, seems to be virtually irrelevant to the contemporary scene of this spiritual search. The dismissive or evasive attitude detectable in the response of many church people to the modern, non-aligned, religious phenomena can be attributed to the fear and confusion they face in preaching to those who may give them all due social respect but still regard them as irrelevant to their own spiritual questioning and searching. The

5

great danger of this today is what it has been ever since the Church lost the power of its early novelty – that we end up preaching to the converted. It is then only a small step to preaching in order to convince ourselves that we believe, to convince ourselves that *we* are converted.

The Church, like Jesus, exists for others. Its power and effectiveness exist in direct proportion to its consciousness of itself. Only in this spiritual – to the world, foolish – state of being other-centred can the Church itself truly believe what it is meant to proclaim, because only then will it be in a state of genuinely experiencing, in the centre of its being, the loving dynamic of the Good News. The Church cannot effectively proclaim a past experience – certainly not to such a self-consciously 'modern' society as our own. It can only proclaim what it is in the state of experiencing – or, to put it slightly differently, it can only proclaim what *it is*. This is the condition for the Church recovering its relevance. And this state of being I have been talking of, this state of being other-centred, is, of course, the state of prayer.

At a time of such rapid change and self-contradiction as we have been living through, it is a brave person who would launch out to generalize about the 'state of the Church today' – a Church that contains South American guerilla priests, an international charismatic movement and supporters of Archbishop Lefebvre. People in the Church today are at many different levels of reality. Some have never really been helped to reach any level of genuine or mature Christian experience and have remained preoccupied with the institutional facets of the Church. Others have found the going so tough that they have slipped into a confected non-reality of their own making, the preservation of which absorbs all their energies and faculties. The call of the gospel should call us to an encounter and communion with the wonderful present reality of God's creation redeemed by the sacrificial love of Jesus and interpenetrated with his Holy Spirit. But this reality has so often been missed because the call of the gospel has so often been replaced by religious illusion – whether of a pietistic or intellectual kind.

If it is difficult to make a clear-cut analysis about the Church of today, we can perhaps project forward into a view of the

6

Church of tomorrow (if, that is, we continue on our present course). We will not be surprised to see a Church with few priests and ministers, dwindling congregations, and empty buildings fulfilling social functions that either have less and less relevance or are indistinguishable from those carried out by secular institutions. The prospect is daunting, and, to some, so depressing that they leave the Church, not wanting to be tied to a sinking ship. And those who stay are so often overwhelmed by the administrative functions that are ever more hectically necessary to service a declining institution.

So, at a time when the general consciousness of all human society has never been more keenly tuned towards the basic need of the stabilizing power of the enduring spiritual realities, the Church is turned, not of course totally, but to a quite unacceptable degree, in the opposite direction – towards itself, its image, its problems, its personnel, its structural changes. It is as if a city without electricity was lighting its streets with candles while a great power source lay untapped in its midst which would be able to light up not only the city but the whole of the surrounding countryside. The Church has always tried and is still trying to find the way of uniting itself with this power source. It is in the very nature of the Church to do this, to draw all life to itself as it builds up the body of Christ and prepares for the fullness when all creation will be incorporated in the Church because all will be united to Christ.

The Church has tried but failed to convince most of its contemporaries that it can satisfy their hunger for the experience of Spirit out of the riches of its own life and wisdom. But in its attempt it has revealed that what it has to do is not merely to *say* something or *do* something but fully to *be* something. The Church must know itself with a joyfulness of self-knowledge that produces the right frequency and draws into itself the scattered signals of its lost contemporaries. That frequency is no less a thing than the life of the Risen Lord, vital in the heart of every being and drawing all being into conscious awareness of itself. The Church is what knows this life at the very centre of its being, which is in harmony with the centre of all being. The visible and multifaceted Church is, therefore, the visible form of the glorified, universal Lord Jesus. The

7

frequency of Christ the person. It is a personal communication made with the authority of *real knowledge*.

It is for knowledge of this intimate and authentic kind that our contemporaries are seeking. And they do search for this far more seriously than for the pleasure-trips and hallucinogenic 'experience' – those superficial newsworthy phenomena which the media encourage us to identify with the religious conscious-ness of our time. Of course, distortion can easily take place. The search for knowledge – the kind of knowledge St Paul was constantly exhorting the early Church to acquire and deepen – begins with a good and pure intention but it also requires a serious readiness for the discipline, patience and ascesis which the search requires. The word *guru* means 'one who is steady' and it is this quality of steadiness, stability and the weight of wise experience that are needed if the search for the spiritual reality is to be successfully concluded, and if, as St Paul put it, we are to run the race and win the prize. The deep religious awareness of our time recognizes this – hence the search for gurus at home and abroad. But where is the Church's guidance, its steadiness, stability, wisdom and its experience of the ever-present power of *the* guru, the Lord himself?

The spiritual climate of our day is made up of both the searching hunger for an absolute knowledge and a deep intuition of the mystery of the *personal* nature of this knowl-edge. It is not a knowledge that can be gained in the same way we acquire the knowledge of history or thermo-dynamics. It is not the knowledge of a 'course on prayer'. These are accretions to our memory banks, possessions, that do not fully partake of the mystery of our personhood. The real knowledge we speak of is different. The centre of consciousness, the intelligent agent is not ourselves acquiring, savouring, experiencing and observ-ing. This knowledge is not something we possess but something that possesses us. We know fully only when we have been fully understood. To *know* in the Christian sense is to be taken up into the mystery of Christ's self-knowledge: his prayer.

The strange and redeeming feature of our rather mad world is that it has been led to this most sensitive and beautiful. spiritual perception. A culture that has almost lost its literacy and its potential for intelligent communication has somehow managed to grasp with a finer sureness than many preceding generations a truth that can only very tenuously be glimpsed between the letters of a word and the backwash of its meaning. It is a perception that has given an often anomalous wisdom to many of the young who are searching for the way to its full meaning. In what other time would Thomas Merton's book *Zen and the Birds of Appetite* have become a bestseller among the young? At what other time have so many focused so fearlessly on the central tenet of Jesus' message – that he who would find his life must lose it?

I may seem to have moved rather too quickly from the dismal prospect for the Church of tomorrow to the spiritual sensitivity of the world of today. To explain where I think the redeeming encounter between the two will eventually take place, let me return to the Church of today and look at some of its more hopeful signs. Because, after all, if we see ahead of us a Church as broken and impotent as it could institutionally become, then that cannot be the Church guided by the Spirit and founded on the rock of Christ. The Church is oceanic. It rises and swells in one place, receding in another. Those who have left self behind to follow Christ have left the shore and are carried on the ocean and moved by the tide and the groundswell.

The signs of hope in today's Church are those features of it that correspond to the religious, spiritual consciousness of today's world – and which therefore put the Church on the wave length of its contemporaries. I have suggested that this can be thought of as consisting of two deeply-rooted preoccupations: the first with the human hunger for true knowledge, the second with the necessity for discovering and fulfilling the personal.

The great prayer-movement that has arisen in the Church on every continent testifies to both of these inner drives. They have not taken on standardized forms of expression and yet remain open and receptive to each other and to the world around them. The charismatic groups and the contemplative houses of prayer point in different ways to the same phenomenon. To many of the young impelled by a spiritual hunger the new Christian communities of prayer are providing real possibilities for being true to their vocation, their pilgrimage –

very often after they have begun to despair of finding a teacher and community where they could be sane, serious and true to their inner drive. This, at least, has been our experience in our monastic meditation centre in London and in our Benedictine Community in Montreal.

The significance is evident of these new communities of prayer which are rediscovering the richness of the Christian tradition of contemplative prayer. Its relevance for all serious people is urgent.

More significant than we perhaps imagine are the great Christian personalities of our day – men and women like Mother Teresa, Cardinal Suenens, Jean Vanier: people whose enthusiasm (in the original sense of the word) transcends sectarian division and nationalism. They testify to the central tenet of Christian conviction and experience: that once the inner commitment – or, in the old language, conversion – has taken place we are en route for the fulfilment, not the eradication, of our personhood: that, once we have lost our life, we do, indeed, find it. They remind us, too, of Jesus' assurance that he came to bring us 'life and life in all its fullness'. It is this that our contemporaries are longing to believe and to experience for themselves.

The Church is bound to help them do just that. But it is so easy for us to talk about 'the Church' fatalistically in the language of politics, history or sociology – as if we were mere observers or victims of the great events which affect us. Modern men and women always tend to see themselves either as an anonymous part of the pattern unfolded to them daily in the newspapers and on the television or, perhaps more insidiously, as the impartial observer, the universal journalist or commentator.

The immediate task for the contemporary Christian is for each of us to see and experience ourselves as the Church we speak of. For each one of us to know ourselves as the presence of the living Christ in our world. This is just the consciousness and response of the great personalities I have mentioned in the particular situation and responsibilities they found themselves in. We have to learn not to see the Church any longer as some multinational company or international organization. But if we are truly to know it as the living Body of Christ of which we are the living cells alive with the life of Christ, then we must rediscover and re-experience ourselves as *persons*, personal witnesses and personal temples of the Spirit. To cease objectifying the Church, externalizing it from ourselves, and to begin seeing it as congruous with our own personal life means that if we examine the role and the nature of the Church today, we are examining the role and nature that *we* have in the concrete world we inhabit.

And so, if the Church is failing to respond to the deep religious needs of our contemporaries it is because, for some reason, we, its people and ministers are failing in our personal response to Christ. Without the life-force of this response which has to originate in our deepest selves, without the confidence, authority and boldness it carries with it, we can only fail to proclaim Christ to all people.

The mystery of the Church as the Body of Christ is the mystery of personhood. That mystery exerts such a force upon us that we are each drawn to live the fullness of the Christ life in our own time and place, to deepen our experience and capacity for experience in every one of our human faculties, to have our eyes opened onto the beauty and power of humanity and the whole of creation in its progress towards its common source and goal. In being thus transformed – 'inwardly renewed day by day', as St Paul expressed it – we become *personally* joined to Christ. We pulsate with his life and at the same time discover our communion with all those who have gone before and all those who will come after us and who are open to the salvific, redeeming love of Jesus. The mystery is Jesus: risen, glorious, fully alive. It is a living mystery that overflows the normal demarcations of our thought and feeling and that transcends the capacity of human structure or organization to contain or direct it. It is a mystery that contains us – a cosmic mystery beyond our comprehension, but *not* beyond our experience.

It is this last conviction – that we can experience this power – that drives on our contemporaries to search for this experience in the East. 'People are changed here on earth by the first resurrection that enlightens them for conversion; in it they pass from death to life . . . ', wrote St Fulgentius of Ruspe. The first resurrection experience is finding our own harmony within and beyond ourselves. It is because this is the realm of mystery that we must allow its power to enter us, or emerge from within us, at the deepest level of our being, beyond cognition, beyond thought. We have to travel to the bedrock of our being where we are, by nature, open to what St Paul calls in Ephesians 'the fullness of God himself'. At this level of our existence, we come into being out of the effulgence of the creative love of God and there we are consciously open to its fullness because we are 'created in its image'. The reawakening spiritual sensitivity of our contemporaries should lead us to listen to this prayer of St Paul with deeper awareness:

> May he grant you strength and power through his Spirit in your inner being, that through faith Christ may dwell in your hearts with love. With deep roots and firm foundations, may you be strong to grasp with all God's people what is the breadth and length and height and depth of the love of Christ and to know it though it is beyond knowledge. So may you attain to fullness of being, the fullness of God himself.[1]

When the early Church proclaimed the Good News like this it proclaimed the power and strength at work within us. That power and strength is Jesus dwelling in our hearts in love. The Christian experience is to discover this power and strength in our inmost being.

In other words, the compelling power of the gospel is an *opportunity* that dawns upon us, and an *invitation* to break through the egotistic barriers of our life, a summons to discover who we are and to become the person we are called to be: and all this by experiencing the life and power of the Lord Jesus at work, active, energizing us in our own heart. When a young person is searching for their own identity and does this with a basic sincerity that ignores sectarian divisions, it is the responsibility of the Church to place this search in the context of the ultimate spiritual reality for mankind – the Christian mystery.

1. Eph. 3:17–19. (Most of the biblical quotations in this book are taken from, or based on, the New English Bible.)

12

We must show this mystery as the culmination of the human spirit.

The Church does this by communicating the life it experiences, not in the first place by any dialectic. This may seem hard to us trained as we are in the supremacy of the ongoing dialectic, but listen to Ephesians again:

> He put everything in subjection beneath his feet and appointed him as supreme head to the Church, which is his body and as such holds within it the fullness of him who receives the entire fullness of God.[2]

The Christian experience St Paul testifies to is not a conceptual one, nor is it principally communicated by the Church on the conceptual level where we can so easily become 'morbidly keen on mere verbal questions and quibbles'.[3]

The experience is best described as a transformation of consciousness, which St Paul called the Christian possessing of the 'mind of Christ'. The communication is spiritual and direct. The Church is consciously present in time and in society when we as members of the Body are experiencing this transformation of consciousness and are in communion with the power and glory of Christ at work within us. When in fact not theory we experience his love at work in our hearts.

Christians are often very nervous in using this kind of language – and understandably so! This is not the way most of us are trained to think of ourselves or the Church. The Church used to be regarded as a kind of pre-programmed computer that gave all the answers if you knew how to present your question – that is, either in scholastic or fundamentalist terms! Much of the contraction that the Church has suffered in recent years is really due to this way of seeing it, which is anathema to those in conscious revolt against those forces in our society which threaten to mechanize and depersonalize human beings. The essence of the truly religious response and the constant challenge the religious man or woman faces is not to retreat from the spiritual and the personal, not to break our basic

2. Eph. 1:22.
3. 1 Tim. 6:4.

covenant which is our creative relationship with God who is Spirit. The hazard of idolatry is just this preference for the mechanical and the legalistic: the preference, in fact, for dull repetition over against the dynamic of conversion. The call of Jesus is to worship the God who is Spirit 'in spirit and in truth':

> But the time approaches, indeed it is already here when those who are real worshippers will worship the Father in spirit and in truth. God is Spirit and those who worship him must worship in spirit and in truth.[4]

I have spoken so far of the deep religious hunger and spiritual sensitivity of our day. I think it could best be described in these words of Jesus, words we have perhaps listened to as an injunction but which we should now be hearing as a declaration of liberty. The great yearning in the hearts of men and women all over the world is for just this experience of worship *in spirit and in truth*. Their hunger is to encounter the mystery of being at its deepest where it is supremely personal. The search is for an authentic experience of ourselves as the created, the loved and the redeemed of God.

In the past we have approached this area, which is the essence of the Christian message, almost wholly in theological or metaphysical terms, that is in an abstract impersonal way. Even in terms of the theology we have used we have failed to achieve the necessary theological equilibrium and the proper perspective of the transcendence and the immanence of God. The shift of religious interest to the East in our time has been an attempt to restore this balance by returning to an apprehension of the immanent God which has always been more characteristic of Eastern than Western religions. There is no doubt that the hunger of our own time is for the God within. And at this moment in history we have an altogether special opportunity to understand the words of Jesus:

> Your Advocate, the Holy Spirit, whom the Father will send

4. Jn. 4:23.

in my name, will teach you everything, and will call to mind all that I have told you.[5]

The power, the momentum, the authoritative and authentic joy of the early Church derived from just this 'well-informed' experience of the immanence of God which we call the indwelling of the Holy Spirit. Now this was an intoxicating experience as the written records proclaim. But more than intoxication or enthusiasm it was an experience so profoundly *personal* to those who were open to it that it wholly rearranged the patterns of observable reality for the enlightened heart and mind:

> When anyone is united to Christ there is a new world (a new creation), the old order has gone and a new order has already begun.[6]

The relevance of this witness of the early Christians for ourselves is that it was not an other-worldly or world-rejecting experience. It was much more an experience of the deeper significance of the whole of creation which was now seen to be interpenetrated with the power of Christ's saving love

> that the universe, all in heaven and on earth might be brought into a unity in Christ.[7]

The experience made it possible to grasp hold of the absolute, transcendent reality and, in doing so, to discover the truly personal identity immanent in mankind and the world. This supreme personal resolution is Jesus. It is the search of our time for *the absolute and the personal* in an integral harmony.

The Church has always been truest to itself and at its most powerful in its direct proclamation of the Kingdom of God within us – a proclamation that invites us to discover who we are. In *De Vera Religione* (1:39), for example, St Augustine put it with felicitous clarity in terms few of the young today would find any difficulty in understanding in their original sense:

> One underestimates self-knowledge if one considers it idle,

5. Jn. 14:26.
6. 2 Cor. 5:17.
7. Eph. 1:10.

quietistic or pietistic. No one remains quite what he was when he knows himself.

'Know thyself' is of course one of the oldest religious slogans, unfortunately also one of the least observed – most religious slogans are. But it is a question of crucial significance for any attempt to reconcile the spiritual sensitivity of our non-Christian society with the Church. In theology we encounter the same problems in terms of 'high' or 'low' Christology. But most theological discussion is largely irrelevant to our contemporaries unless they have themselves experienced the power of the gospel of Christ personally and had it effectively communicated to them with authority. Much of the suffering and confusion associated with the spiritual searching of our contemporaries is due to the fact that it is so intuitive and remains unarticulated and poorly understood. This is the opportunity for the Church to identify the unknown forces at work and to show, in living example rather than conceptual theory, that the goal towards which these forces are driving is, within the Christian experience, known territory. People today are looking for the perennial fruits of the Spirit: peace, liberty, joy, the freedom and power to love. Above all, they are seeking the courage and strength to *be*. We are all aware with a peculiar insight that for. this discovery we must come to terms with ourselves at our simplest, our most elemental. This is the preliminary work we must all undertake. As St Augustine put it, *Man must first be restored to himself, make of himself a stepping-stone and rise from self to God.*

Serious men and women see this clearly in our own time and share a universal awareness – or an instinct striving to become awareness – that the matter is both urgent and personally challenging. To undertake the work we have to call in aid all our own native resources as well as the accumulated experience of all people. If today's pilgrims are not turning to the Christian tradition it must surely be due in large part to their failing to see among us enough men and women who have evidently been restored to themselves and who therefore know the urgency and the personal dimension of the pilgrimage. We have the gospel – the inspired Word of God – but unless the Word

16

has inspired us to leave self behind and to follow the light of Christ as his intimate disciple, then we cannot hand on the gospel with its living, true, and effective power. The Church, as the Body of Christ, as his personal presence among people, is so constituted that the gospel without the authenticating elements of personal verification is a dead letter.

The gospel demands more of us the longer we live it. The inner commitment and personal surrender involved in the Christian pilgrimage takes us into ever deeper realms of being. The work of entering into these realms where we become more suffused with the light of Christ transforms what we once suffered into what we now enjoy. When all has been said – and after all not very much can be said or at least said very well, it can only be known and shared – the essence of the pilgrimage is the loss of our self in order to discover our true personhood – a personhood that is found in the person of the glorified Lord. We are not called to be slaves or sycophants or flunkeys in regard to the gospel, but free people proclaiming a truth greater than ourselves which we have experienced in our inmost being.

We are called to be a people of knowledge who have become full persons. In answering this call we are empowered to answer the call of our contemporaries for guidance, inspiration, above all for *knowledge of the Truth*. Much of our reluctance to answer this call in the past has been due to a reluctance to make the complete commitment of ourselves to the pilgrimage. We have opted for a comfortable social role rather than for an open, dynamic personal relationship. The climate of our day is a climate of prayer, a hunger for a personal encounter with the absolute and a realization of the personal. The Church in its human modality is witnessing this same hunger with all its attendant upheaval and restructuring of priorities. But it is not enough to regard ourselves as merely reflecting a universal phenomenon. The Church *shares* but because its centre of consciousness, its heart, is greater than itself it also leads. *O Christian recognize your dignity*. The Church is called to teach and at no other time has its teaching been more urgently needed. It does not teach through committees or organizations or reports and manifestos. It teaches through persons. It

17

teaches through us – provided that we have seriously set foot on the pilgrimage and begun our personal encounter with the Master.

Christian Community and the University

I said earlier that I thought the spiritual atmosphere of our own time could be described in terms of a reawakening to the values of the absolute and the personal. And I went on to say that I thought that if the Church were to fulfil its task of completing all spiritual consciousness in itself, then it would have first of all to see the times as they really are – that is, be true to its own *prophetic character*. And secondly, it would have to manifest in itself, through a network of personal relationships, that the resolution of the absolute and the personal has already been accomplished in Jesus and that *this* is the Christian mystery – for the Church must be true too to her *priestly character*.

I would like to descend from the abstraction of this sort of language and relate what I have been saying to the concrete situation of the University Chaplaincy. It would be most arrogant of me to try to set out within the confines of a single paper a sure-fire methodology for contemporary campus ministry: the more so as I have never myself exercised such a ministry. What I offer you now are some thoughts for your consideration that follow on from what I had to say to you earlier about the contemporary climate for prayer.

Arnold Toynbee saw the main event of the twentieth century as the encounter between the Eastern and Western religious traditions. The present attraction of the East for the young is that in Buddhism, Hinduism or Zen the priority of the real experience is put before them in all simplicity and frankness – with none of the embarrassment or confusion with which we in the West so often talk of spiritual experience. The same concern is evident in many of the Christian revival movements among the young where the central preoccupation is the verifiable and verifying *experience* of conversion, of 'finding Jesus'. In any religious discussion with the young it soon becomes clear that the word 'experience' has greater force and significance than the word 'faith'. We are a more sceptical age than many others but, in some ways, more child-like: we will believe only what we have experienced. We can go forward trustingly into the dark only if we have had an experience of the light first. This, I think, is one of the great signs of the integrity of the spiritual consciousness of our time.

The young look to the East because they see the possibility of an experience of God's actual presence in his world; that is, of an absolute and authenticating dimension that subsists in all things and maintains the essential harmony between mankind and matter. But the experience for which they are seeking is also one of knowing this absolute in direct, intimate relation to themselves, not as a conceptual reality known only as part of a moral system tied to social relativities, but as an inner *personal* relationship. Out of this experience develops a full acceptance of their own personhood and knowledge of their own place in the world: who they are and where they are going. The balance and harmony with God and themselves for which they are seeking is affirmed in the words of Jesus:

You must therefore be all goodness just as your heavenly Father is all good.[8]

One of the most important perceptions to which our religious instinct has now led our society is that this type of truly religious experience cannot be encountered merely by being a part of an *organization*. The young, in particular, have come to understand the role of the teacher as an experienced guide and animator, and one of their first instincts, as we have plenty of evidence for today, is to look for a teacher and a community within which to tread the path of their pilgrimage. One of the major tragedies of our situation is that there are so few teachers of that goodness which Jesus enjoined upon us, so few who can speak of goodness out of their own experience.

The instinct which leads people today to look for a teacher

8. Mt. 5:48.

is not a new one. It is an essential part of our religious and spiritual make-up. The whole New Testament is a testimony to the need for enlightened teachers, people whose personal experience allows them to transcend a sense of egotistic identity and enter into a loving relationship with individuals for the sake of the advancement of the Kingdom.

> You heard my teachings in the presence of many witnesses; put that teaching into the charge of people you can trust, such as will be competent to teach others.[9]

One of the great revelations to which the newly awakened consciousness of our day can lead us is to read the letters of St Paul in this light and to see to what a deep degree he was the teacher of these early Churches, planting the seed of the Word, cultivating it and ever encouraging them to persevere on their pilgrimage to the full knowledge of the Spirit to which they were called.[10] The anger of Jesus with the Pharisees in chapter twenty-three of Matthew is aroused because they were betraying the trust with which they were invested as teachers of the people. Rather than leading them to the light of spiritual maturity, the Pharisees were themselves blind guides leading people on false paths. And not only did they remain outside the sanctuary of truth themselves but they made themselves stumbling blocks to prevent others from entering.

The ministry of Jesus was that of a teacher, one who was leading those who freely followed him on the pilgrimage to that same experience he himself had been led to. Chapter six of Matthew and chapter eleven of Luke show him giving specific direction on prayer in response to a particular request. Although he healed and listened he was, to his contemporaries, someone more than a counsellor or miracle worker. He was a teacher leading them in *love* to the experience of their own goodness as children of God and to a *mature* relationship with himself. In reporting his last discourses to his disciples, John shows us to what level of being the Master had been leading them: not infantile dependence, but a fully human, loving relationship:

9. 2 Tim. 2:2.
10. 1 Cor. 3:1–10.

You are my friends if you do what I command you. I call you servants no longer; a servant does not know what his master is about. I have called you friends because I have disclosed to you everything that I heard from my Father. You did not choose me; I chose you. I appointed you to go and bear fruit, fruit that shall last.[11]

Monasticism developed in the Church from a consciousness of the need for this fundamental relationship. In part the monastic movement grew out of a deep discontent with the formalism and secularism into which the now officially-recognized Church had declined and so it represented a return to the simplicity and direct experience of the primitive Church. It also manifested an understanding of the need of individuals for teachers of prayer. Many of these features of the era of early monasticism can be seen at work in our own day: the breakdown of traditional institutional structures, radical insecurity about the future, an upheaval in social moral values. Curiously enough, our response is along similar lines. The new forms of community which are developing within and without religious orders are similar movements towards finding the balance, wisdom and encouragement on the spiritual pilgrimage that only a teacher and community can give.

The operative word is *balance*. No community can lose sight of the fact that its goal is also its Teacher, the magnetic force that draws people to itself along a path of his choosing, not theirs. But within this scheme a visible teacher is needed to encourage, inspire and to help create an atmosphere of love and so enkindle a spirit of selflessness that is the only sane milieu for perseverance. He or she is a visible sign, and in this sense a creator of inner stability and a lack of self-centredness. Augustine Baker, who represents the spirit of English Benedictinism, had a typical English suspicion of those who attracted attention to themselves. He concluded his own teaching on prayer and the need for a teacher like this:

The director is not to teach his own way or indeed any determinate way of prayer but to instruct his disciples how

11. Jn. 15:15–17.

they may themselves find out the way proper to them. In a word, he is only God's usher and must lead souls in God's way not his own.

The Church of our own day is beginning to rediscover these essential elements of healthy Christian community. One of the strangest experiences of travelling in the world today is to meet with the same newly-awakened perceptions about the need for teachers and community developing in different ways in every part of the universal Church. I think that what we are seeing anew is that the basic unit for proclaiming the gospel is a living Christian community. Ministers of the gospel only really make sense when they proclaim the Word from within the assembly of those redeemed by Jesus. Paradoxically, therefore, their first task is to create the community that will be the basis of their ministry.

To be effective and credible, this community has also to be forged together in some common and enduring spiritual experience. In other words, it must have essentially the same way of apprehending the spiritual reality. In each member of the community there must be a serious commitment to the deepening of their own personal experience. There must also be a double sense of responsibility: in the first place, each must understand their need of the encouragement, support and love of the community; in the second, each must be aware of their own importance for providing encouragement, support and love to others.

One of the saddest and most damaging forces in religion is that of the community that exists merely for the selfish interests of its own members, for their own mutual convenience. Not a few attempts at religious community are made on this basis. In failing to lead its members to a deeper religious experience, they create an inverted power, a force of self-rejection that hardens the barriers of ego and so becomes entirely counter-productive, a counter-sign. The religious instinct, no less than other human instincts, is easily distorted and can be turned against a person or community rather than leading towards self-transcendence. The teacher has a special responsibility for avoiding this within his or her community and does so, as St

Benedict understood in his description of the ideal abbot, both by having something to teach and by loving every member of the community to the fullness of their capacity.

One of the early desert fathers asked a searching question to illustrate the superiority of community life over the eremitical: 'If you are on your own, whose feet can you wash?' The community provides an opportunity for incarnating the love that underlies, permeates and inspires each individual's pilgrimage to the source of that love in his or her own heart. Turned away from themselves towards each other, they are turned towards that ultimate Other who dwells in their inmost being. A community rooted in this Christ-event of otherness as a living, a present reality opens the possibility of sharing the experience of our redemption by the love of Jesus. It is this participation that creates and strengthens Religious, Christian, Community. It also bears witness to the world: *See how these Christians love one another.*

The college campus affords a particularly fertile ground for the realization of the ideals and the fulfilment of the Christian evangelical imperative. So many of the young today are in a condition of expectation, searching and longing. They are often hampered in their search by the feeling that their condition is unique and so often miss the opportunity of discovery when it occurs simply for lack of any articulate sense of what they really *are* looking and waiting for. The Church, as it is incarnated on the campus, has the opportunity and the mission to enter into sympathetic understanding with this type of confusion. It does so by using the power with which she is invested to lead people out of confusion into clarity, from darkness into the light and from their restricted self-consciousness to the liberty that flows from discovering the power of the gospel within.

What we want to offer them is this – not, primarily, classes on Scripture, nor, in the first place, discussions on ethics, or lectures on modern theology – but something more serious and more enduring than anything that can be contained in any theological lecture. We want to lead them, rather, to understand that the genuine power, authority and self-verification they seek are to be encountered on the truly personal level within a truly Christian community. Many groups go by the name of 'community' which lack any real communion at any serious level and so I think that when we talk about 'religious community' we should be careful to distinguish between the club, the organization, the sodality and what does truly merit the name 'community'. The difference is twofold: in the type of relationship between the members and in the group's relationship and attitude with the rest of society. The club is typically characterized by the fact that a group of people have found some common interest or concern. It may be curling, the art of debating or acting, the poetry of Horace or of Wallace Stevens or an interest in religion. Sharing at this level of our life is, of course, vital. The vitality of our culture depends upon it. But, inevitably, a group thus organized around a common interest will be defined over-against those outside their circle whose areas of interest are different. There is, therefore, something inherently exclusive about any group that is not, truly, a community.

Many Christian organizations on small and large scales are better described as groups than communities. The area of common concern or interest may be genuine enough: in Scripture, in social work, in political action. But the level of shared experience between the members is not deep enough to allow for the development of real communion. The only level that *is* deep enough is not that of scholarship, ethics or politics but that of the Spirit. And it is only at that level that the group's relationship with the larger social reality around it becomes truly welcoming, *inclusive*, embracing, loving. How often have we encountered Christian groups that come to cultivate themselves as an elite set apart from the profane world about them which they presume to judge and condemn?

The nature of any particular community is decided by the common experience that binds its members together in mutual obedience and receptiveness. In a religious community that experience must be *religious*. And when a community has learned to share and deepen its spiritual experience together in easy commerce it has discovered a dimension in the lives of its members, its common life, that takes them outside the narrow limits of any distinct group. Then they begin to develop an apprehension of the fraternity all people share at the basic level of all human experience: the level of the Spirit.

And so the type of community I would see as providing the Christian presence and witness on a modern campus would be a truly *religious* community. It would not be a specialist sect cultivating its own erudition or perfection but a group of really human persons in the process of experiencing their full humanity in the light of the Christian mystery. Their prayer would be an embracing of the world about them, *Christian and non-Christian*, because it would afford the courage that is the essential dynamic of love, the courage to embrace what is different to ourselves and in the embrace to recognize it as one with ourselves. In the past, we have too often made the mistake of understanding the ongoing process of redemption as a vertical movement travelling downwards. We have failed to understand the apostolate of redemption by which we co-redeem with Christ but only by loving those who are unredeemed because love has not yet reached into their inmost being. The precondition for redemption is union, an encounter on the same level, the level of our common humanity.

This of course all depends upon the quality of life and personhood of the members of the community. But then does not the Church depend on this too? The crucial point is that this necessary quality of life is not conceptual but experiential. A group may be articulate and well-informed, ready to discuss and accept criticism and still lack the necessary quality of having actually experienced the love of Christ at the level of their being which is beyond thought and word.

The New Testament is constantly reminding us that the experience of the love of God in Jesus Christ is a transcendent experience: we must know it, though it is beyond knowledge, eye has not seen it nor heart conceived of it.

The fatal temptation to which we are all prone to succumb is to talk about 'transcendence' so much and so well that we become 'intoxicated by the exuberance of our own verbosity' – as Gladstone once remarked to Disraeli. The danger is that we can end by believing that we have solved the *problem* of transcendence and yet be far from having experienced the *mystery*. When this begins to happen we are in fact dissipating rather than communicating the mystery and are left holding what T.S. Eliot called 'receipts for deceits', dull platitudes that convince no one, hardly (after a while) even ourselves.

What is the element necessary to preserve and refine our apprehension of the mystery of the love of Christ at work within us? It is simply silence. And it is this understanding that has led so many today to the threshold of real prayer. They are waiting on that threshold, waiting to be led by the Church into the experience to which the Lord God leads all. The Church's role is to remind them of the essentially transcendent nature of their pilgrimage and to teach them not to underestimate the wonder of our vocation or to oversimplify the means of realizing it.

There is a real sense (and it is this understanding from the East, from Zen in particular, that has attracted so many of the young) in which it is not even appropriate to the transcendent nature of the mystery to talk of *experiencing* it at all. It is so utterly different from something we can savour for our own enjoyment on our own terms. But many of the young have been misled on this question and have come to think in materialistic terms of their spiritual pilgrimage, asking all the time 'What am *I* getting out of it?' Here too the Church has an urgent message to deliver. It can only deliver it though by incarnating the pilgrimage in communities seriously committed to a daily openness to the mystery of God's love *flooding our inmost heart*. The expression is that of St Paul writing to the Romans. The effectiveness of his message lay in communicating the truly self-transcending dynamic of the Christian mystery which is what it means to be creatively annihilated by God's loving power:

I live no longer but Christ lives in me.[12]

He communicated this experience not merely as his own but as one to which we are all summoned:

so that we also might set our feet upon the path of new life.[13]

12. Gal. 2:20.
13. Rom. 6:4.

It seems to me that the campus minister, too, must be above all one who speaks with the authority of his or her own experience of what it is to be *alive to God in union with Christ Jesus*. The basis of this authority is the important question he or she has to face. As all Christians must.

The basis is not, first of all, any cult of personality. The men or women who preach the gospel are not preaching themselves or even using their own power to preach. The Christian witness is called to an experience of total immersion in the power and affirming love of God out of which they emerge as someone different and yet more themselves than they ever were. They are beyond vanity because their source of joy is the proclamation of something other than themselves. They are beyond doubt because their experience of the reality of their own being in Christ has touched their inmost heart and the pressure of that encounter can never be removed. They are beyond timidity because the power of the love of God is constantly being renewed and constantly taking them beyond themselves.

This other-centredness of the awakened Christian is not, strictly speaking, just the condition *for* prayer. It is essentially the condition *of* prayer, the state of prayer itself. It will always be accompanied by a personal commitment to the *daily experience of prayer* as a total turning of the whole person towards God, aside from all distraction and all activity, everything that is not concentrated solely upon God. Such a Christian is fulfilling St Paul's injunction to 'pray without ceasing' because the inner eye of his or her consciousness has been opened by redemptive contact with Christ's love and is permanently attentive to his indwelling presence. Thus every Christian is called to be a person of prayer.

The campus ministers have this calling in a particularly urgent area of education and training. They do not need to be primarily people of learning or organization, but in this full sense of the word, they need to be people of prayer. As people who are preaching the gospel of other-centredness, they themselves must be already on the pilgrimage that this gospel requires us to tread.

In treading this pilgrimage and proclaiming this gospel with the necessary confidence and assurance, they are not pointing to themselves but to the Truth and the Way that has possessed them. This other-centredness is the only way to follow Christ with seriousness of purpose and maturity of spirit. Christ was himself radically other-centred. He drew his power and inspiration from the Father and discovered that empowering compound of sincerity and authenticity that only love, selflessness, other-centredness can create:

> I do not speak on my own authority, but the Father who sent me has himself commanded me what to say and how to speak. I know that his commands are eternal life. What the Father has said to me, therefore, that is what I speak.[14]

The message *we* have been commanded to deliver, to repeat with all the freshness that the creative Spirit imbues us with, is of immense and contemporary urgency, most of all perhaps for the young. But it is a hard message, a hard saying, and it can barely be heard let alone accepted unless we ourselves are the living witnesses of its authenticity. Conceptually, we can talk about it in any number of ways – the discovery of our personhood, an encounter with the absolute, have been the terms I have been using. I think these can find responsive echoes in contemporary thought and language. But the conceptual is no substitute for the practical. And in practical terms our message is a call to the *rediscovery of prayer* and of ourselves as having the capacity for deep prayer in spirit and in truth, of prayer as the central authenticating fact of our life and personhood.

I think we can state the message like this: The search of all people in every age has been a search for some ultimate *meaning* perceptible among all the complexities and paradoxes of life. It is also a search for some ultimate *authority* in whom and on whom we can place complete reliance and certainty without losing our human self-respect or integrity. Idolatry and mere religiosity have only ever provided temporary satisfaction for this search. Our particular message which we have received by the manifold disclosure of God's self-revelation that culminates in the person of Jesus is that these ultimate goals of

14. Jn. 12:49–50.

meaning and authority are to be found within the depths of the human soul – within the mystery of our own personhood. It is the treasure buried in the field of our own heart. It is at this depth that we make contact with the infinite, or rather that the infinite rushes up to make contact with us. And everyone has this potential, the capacity to effect the contact between the finite and the infinite and to be redeemed and glorified in that loving fusion. The reason for this is simply that we exist. And that we can learn to exist with complete simplicity. The reason is that God *is*: and that, as we learn through Jesus, with him and in him, God dwells in our hearts in love.

No one can plumb these depths out of mere curiosity or desire. It is not, in this sense, an experience like any other experience, or perhaps an *experience* at all. Because in prayer we are not seeking to experience the experience but simply to know with the *knowledge* that is wholly at one with *being*. This blissful equilibrium between knowing and being is the consciousness that allows us to know ourselves as created in the image of God. It is the knowledge by which we are known. And so, to those who have already started out on the pilgrimage of meditation or are trying to be faithful to it, the Church can now bring the message that will show them just what the path is and to what it is leading them.

In order to follow this pilgrimage to our heart we have to transcend all division. We do not begin by trying to see the 'harmony of the Cosmos'. We begin by passing beyond all dividedness in ourselves, the division between knowledge and being that we call self-consciousness, self-fixation, the division between self and other that we call desire.

In overcoming these inner divisions and in passing beyond the old self, we transcend movement. We discover unity in stillness. We understand the injunction of the psalmist: *Be still and know that I am God*. This is the path of meditation that leads to the discovery of the prayer of Jesus in our heart, the path to the ultimate, the only and the ever-present reality. Where teachers are urgently needed is in preparing people to dispose themselves patiently and perseveringly, but also with an ever-deepening joy, for this reality. It is the teacher, in particular, who helps the community to establish and be faithful to a new hierarchy of values by which it can surrender trivial concerns for the ultimate concern and also to recognize the moments of choice and the opportunities for growth that confront us, when they occur.

People are particularly open to the spiritual dimension of their life in their youth. They are particularly open at that time of youth when they are both opening themselves to the circumstances of life that challenge their maturity and also learning the essential discipline that must accompany all progress and relationships. If so many are learning these lessons badly it is in large part due to the fact that an essential part of their intuition, the spiritual, is not being properly developed. The years of college education form a period of unusual vulnerability but a period, also, of unique opportunity.

The opportunity for the campus minister is to create a living Christian community which exists primarily for the personal realization of the Kingdom in the hearts of its members. From the serious commitment that demands will spring the living, personal witness to Christ for the world around it. In their shared openness to the reality of the Indwelling Spirit, an openness sustained and deepened by fidelity to regular meditation and to prayer together, they will manifest the basic truth of the Christian message. This is the truth that joy springs from seriousness, liberty from discipline, self-fulfilment from other-centredness.

It is often the discipline that people notice first. This is the fidelity to the regular times of prayer together where each is deepening his or her own openness to the Spirit while also encouraging and sustaining others on their pilgrimage. Such regular discipline is necessary in any community based on respect and love for each other. I have not found either here or in England that any serious-minded person was discouraged from joining such a community because of the discipline involved. Indeed, what I have found is that they have been looking for just such a community where a shared, free discipline testifies to seriousness of purpose and authenticity of experience. Because although we can deliver the message of the gospel with joy and fullness of personal liberty we cannot offer any short cuts. There are none. The call of St Paul and the early Church for discipline and sustained commitment is just as relevant today. And today too there is no more powerful means of preaching the gospel of the Good News than the witness of faithful communities rooted and founded in this commitment. The Christian priority is commitment, community, communication.

Teachers are needed. But teachers cannot be produced for the spiritual pilgrimage of prayer as we can train teachers for our schools within two or three years. The teaching involved is not comparable to any other form of teaching or technique of training. It is not a question of taking a course in techniques of prayer, or of attending seminars on spirituality. The means, context, style and presentation are all in the power of the Lord Jesus, the teacher within. But the teachers-in-community are in a real sense the channel for this power in the initial stages of growth. What they need is the actual experience and knowledge of being on the pilgrimage themselves and of being led thereon by a power within and beyond themselves. It is perhaps better expressed as an absence rather than a possession, an unlearning rather than a skill. It is rather a dissipation of an illusory self which is the breeding-ground of all image-making and power-consciousness. In its place there emerges the 'true self' – the power and love of the Lord working through his disciples.

The teacher both represents and lovingly expresses the pure openness and simplicity of prayer. What he or she has to communicate is nothing less than the actual experience of Jesus awakening to his Father in the full realization of his personhood. The *theology* we have to communicate is that the wonder of the Christian mystery is just this same awakening which occurs in us because Jesus lives in us and because his awakening transports *him and us* outside of time into the eternity of the present moment. This is the knowledge of God in love. Enlightenment with the light and life of Christ is the awakening of Jesus' human consciousness to the fullness of the mystery of God. And it is the self-same enlightenment to be found in our hearts by following the pilgrimage of prayer in meditation. Just as Jesus discovered who he was in this enlightenment, so it is his invitation to us to awaken our personhood within his enlightenment and to know ourselves as the redeemed and loved children of God. In awakening to ourselves we awaken to Jesus, in him and through him, who dwells within us in love and leads us ever closer to the source of all life and being.

Like the disciples on the mountain we fall back in fear at the revelation of this mystery which is the splendour of the Lord Jesus. It is so terribly close to us. But this *is* Christianity – the Christianity we preach and if we play it down we not only betray its truth and urgency, we also fail our contemporaries whom we are charged to inform of the fullness of the gospel message. And this is the very thing that men and women everywhere are looking for: personhood, community, meaning, authority, contact with ultimate reality, perhaps nowhere more urgently today than on the college campus.

The Christian tradition of prayer, of meditation, is incredibly rich but it is a tradition from which our own impoverishment of spiritual experience can seriously alienate us. We are being led back into the heart of this tradition today. Its heart is the living centre of reality, the person of Jesus. The way back is incredibly *simple*. Not *easy* perhaps. But simple because all that is needed for our part is good-will, openness and perseverance. The strength for it all is to be found within the traditional structure of teacher and community.

The urgency of our day is to find our way back to this pilgrimage and to lead others onto it. Its goal is the person of the Lord Jesus fully alive in our hearts and in the hearts of all people. The means he has chosen for finding him is also personal because when we find ourself we find Jesus. We cannot risk again forgetting that the means are not institutional or structural but personal. The disciple, the teacher, the goal is *personal*. The price and reward is our own personhood. In our end is our beginning. Above all and within all Jesus is Lord, absolutely, personally.

The Word is near you: it is upon your lips and in your heart. This means the word of faith which we proclaim. If on your lips is the confession, Jesus is the Lord, and in your heart the faith that God raised him from the dead, then you will find salvation. For the faith that leads to righteousness is in

33

the heart and the confession that leads to salvation is upon the lips.[15]

15. Rom. 10:8–10.

Community of Love

Preface

Every quarter an oblate meeting is held at the Montreal Priory. The following chapters are talks John Main gave at these meetings. An oblate is a member of a monastic community which forms a spiritual family or extended community of the monastery. Oblates are men and women young and old, in all walks of life who share in the life, vision and work of the community. The essential bond is that of meditation but the sense of sharing this spiritual journey may take many forms. Oblates enter the community in a year's novitiate in a simple ceremony held in the monastery or, now, in other designated places. The final step of expressing this sense of shared pilgrimage is the final oblation in which the oblate promises to commit his or her life to God and to the service of the world in the spirit of the Benedictine monastic tradition and the particular community of the monastery.

His deep love of the monastic life was rooted in John Main's understanding of it as a 'sign of the reality of God's presence in the world'. He saw it as something sacred and transcendent. But also as a life lived by human beings who did not put off their human frailties by putting on the habit. This mingling of the sacred and the ordinary constituted the Christian transcendent in monasticism. And also its liberty and joyfulness of spirit.

Liberty and playfulness characterized John Main's own spirit, the fruit of a serene and single-minded commitment to the discipline of the monastic paradigm. He knew it was not the only paradigm of the Christian life. But he knew it as an essential one and that, being of the essence, it was an archetype, a universal model which called forth a response in every spirit that truly seeks God.

He often told oblates of the community how encouraging their response to the Priory's monastic witness was to the monks themselves; how their fidelity and participation to the teaching of meditation and in the work of the monastery inspired the small core of monks to continue deepening their own commitment. The oblate inspired him to clarify and expand his own vision of the new monasticism – a monasticism that would be smaller in numbers, less institutionalized, but more and more purely rooted in its contemplative tradition as a present reality and so forming always more concentrated seeds of spiritual energy in the heart of a turbulent and confused world.

In the faith and courage of his founding the Priory John Main became the monastic witness, the teacher and the prophet that his lifelong discipleship of Christ led him to be. He led the way into a new monasticism that incarnated the gospel paradox of expansion through contraction. By simplifying the monastic life and linking its apostolate directly to meditation – the work is to teach and share that tradition – the community expanded rapidly in a few years. He was, to use a distinction he drew in one of these oblate talks, a heroic leader rather than a father figure. Though he led by love as well as heroic example.

His love for the oblates of the Priory comes through in these talks given on the Sunday afternoon oblate meetings still held every few weeks at the monastery. As their numbers grew and their commitment deepened it became clear that the very old idea of lay-association with a monastic family was taking on a new and vigorous life. As his last illness brought him closer to death the love that was always in him burned more and more intensely. It brought many oblates to him and he died as monastic teachers do with his disciples around him.

He passed beyond the confines of the monastery he founded. He always reminded monks and oblates alike never to make the old error of seeing the monastery as an end in itself. The end of the monastic life is not the monastery but the Kingdom of God. This sense of the transcendent value of monasticism set him free to share it with oblates and so to revivify an ancient form of Christian discipleship. The fruit of his liberty of spirit is his continued presence in the community that gathered round him. The work of the monastery like the growth of the oblate community was not, he insisted, a movement but a fellowship. In these talks to oblates many of the seeds of that fellowship were sown.

Laurence Freeman OSB

Conversion and Transcendence

Just as there is an evil zeal which separates from God and leads to hell so is there a good zeal which separates from evil and leads to God and life everlasting. Let monks, therefore, exercise this zeal with the most fervent love. Let them, that is, give one another honour and precedence. Let them bear with the greatest patience one another's infirmities whether of body or of character and let them vie in paying obedience one to another. Let no one in the monastery follow what seems good for himself but rather let him follow what is good for another. And let the monks practice fraternal charity with a most pure love. Let them fear God. Let them love their abbot with a sincere and humble affection and let them prefer nothing whatsoever to Christ and may he bring us all alike to life everlasting.

(Rule of St Benedict, Chapter 72)

That is one of the great sentences of the Rule. *Let the monk prefer nothing whatsoever to Christ*. The monastic life is a life that witnesses to the absolute value of our whole life centred in Christ. St Benedict knew from his own experience that we cannot find our ultimate centre in the world. Christ is the centre for each of us and for all of us. And St Benedict discovered this from his own experience of monastic life and from his own reflection on the gospel. The world, the old creation, is passing away. Christ the new man endures. And the new creation is for all eternity. And it is now. As St Benedict puts it so clearly in the Rule, the new creation can only be seen with the vision that comes from a pure heart, with the vision that comes from a humble heart. For St Benedict, filled as he was with the spirit of the New Testament, God and only God is to be worshipped, not mammon; not golden calves. God alone is good and loving God, worshipping God is the call to each of us to be open to our own eternal potential in God.

Those who follow the Rule of St Benedict and the spirit of the Rule are those who humbly search for the way to realize their potentiality in God. It seems to me that the supreme importance of the monastic life both for the Church and for the world is that it is a sign of the reality of God's presence in our midst. The message that the monk has to give to the world arises not in the first place from his words but from his life itself. His life has its priorities arranged very simply. And in the first place is his whole-hearted search for God. The effectiveness of the message that he has to give arises from the depth of the personal commitment with which this search is pursued. And that is the power of the Rule of St Benedict for all of us whether we are in the monastic order or whether we associate ourselves with the monastic order. The message that those who follow St Benedict's vision have is the message *Lift up your hearts. Open your eyes to what is eternally real, the new creation and seek the purity of heart that will open your eyes.* What the Benedictine vision has to say above all is *know from your own heart, from your own experience that you were created for infinite expansion of spirit.*

The message of those of us that form the monastic community, monks and oblates, is that these are not just idealistic cries. They are entirely realistic possibilities for each of us if only we are open to the experience of Jesus. If only we are open to the ontological change that took place in Jesus when he rose from the dead and burst the bonds of mankind's slavery, making it possible for each of us to participate in that bursting of bonds. This is the place and purpose of our prayer, to be fully open to the new consciousness of Jesus, his freedom, his liberty, his love of the Father.

St Benedict was clear in the Rule that we must approach the mystery of God not through someone else's witness but through our own experience. He has the monk recite every day, 'Oh that today you would hear his voice. Harden not your heart.' And so, a key personal word in the Rule of St Benedict is the word 'conversion'. As you know, the Christian is one converted to Christ. St Benedict asks us to live this conversion as the main thrust of our life. What does this mean, *conversion*, for us as men and women of the twentieth century? What I would like to put before you now is that I think we can best understand conversion in the vocabulary of the twentieth century if we think of it in terms of *transcendence*. That means the expansion of our being that comes about as we cross the frontiers of our own limitations and leave self behind to cross to the further shore. The whole purpose of the Rule of St Benedict and of monastic life is to leave self behind, to burst the bubble and illusion of egoism. Transcendence is a dynamic motion beyond ourselves in which we leave every limiting factor behind and in the power of Christ enter into a truly creative development of our own being.

I think prayer could be described as transcendence realized. Turning aside from every created thing, we find ourselves in the Creator. And finding ourselves in the Creator we find ourselves in harmony with all creation. For this reason, conversion in the Benedictine vision is not a rejection of the world but a vision of the world in the redemptive light of God's love. As you can hear in that Chapter 72 of the Rule, conversion for Benedict is conversion to the brethren, to think of others before we think of self, conversion to Christ, to prayer and to God in Christ. I think it is of enormous importance for all of us as we begin our monastic life to be clear that everyone of us is called to fullness of being, to the fullness of God himself. What that means is that every one of us is called to know God with God's own self-knowledge. None of us can understand that fully. None of us can understand the magnificence of our vocation as Christians. But we can all enter into the experience of it by knowing God with the human knowledge of Jesus Christ. That is the call of each of us.

St Benedict says in the Prologue to the Rule that in the monastery there must be nothing harsh and nothing burdensome. But the Rule is an eminently practical document. We turn aside from everything that distracts from this fullness of life in God. Benedict tells us that our life, if only we can live the monastic vision, will be filled with joy and we will approach God, not walking but *running* with indescribable joy.

I want to urge all of you to read the Rule every day. This evening the new novices will receive a copy of the Rule. The Rule is divided up, and for each day of the year there is a short section for you to read. When you first read it, it might seem to you that many of the sections have no relevance whatever for you in your life in the world in the twentieth century. But always look behind the words and be open to the spirit. The spirit of the Rule is marvellously human, marvellously compassionate, and wonderfully clear. But if we are serious in our search for God we must be single-minded and whole-hearted. I want to end by reading to you from the Prologue to the Rule:

> Therefore we must establish a school of the Lord's service in founding which we hope to ordain nothing that is harsh or burdensome. But if for good reason, for the amendment of evil habit or for the preservation of charity, there be some strictness of discipline, do not be at once dismayed and run away from the way of salvation of which the entrance must need be narrow. But as we progress in our monastic life and in faith our hearts shall be enlarged and we shall run with unspeakable sweetness of love in the way of God's commandments so that never abandoning his rule but persevering in his teaching in the monastery until death we shall share by patience in the sufferings of Christ so that we may deserve to be partakers also of his Kingdom.

That is the aim and the vision that we put before our new novices.

The Heroic Leader

It is a very important thing for us to have you as our oblates. A community of love (and that is what we are about) has to be something that expands. It isn't something that can just be a completely self-contained unit. And each of you, in your own way, have added a particular and lovely dimension to our community. So we are delighted that we are going to receive the new oblates this afternoon.

I think that what a community is about is *support*. We really do help one another by our love for one another and we feel greatly supported that we have you as our friends, and as our brothers and sisters, because that is what it means to be part of the oblate community of a Benedictine monastery. The brotherhood and sisterhood we share is that we are brethren in the Lord, that it is the Lord Jesus who is our brother and God who is our Father. It is a very marvellous thing that we are able to share that dimension of life with one another.

I thought I would begin this afternoon by just bringing you up to date on our community news. One of the best kept secrets in Montreal is that we are shortly to move from this house to a new home because of a really astonishing benefaction that we have received. We have been given a lovely house and three and a half acres of gardens by the McConnell Foundation. The daughter of J.W. McConnell, who built the house, called to see us in June and said that the Foundation would like to donate it to our community. I have been thinking – and as you know St Benedict is very keen on humility – that if my cause for canonization is ever introduced we can put forward as one of the miracles of our foundation that we were given this house in this quite unpredictable way. I hope that we will have our next meeting there and I think you will all agree that it will provide a perfect context for our work and for our life, because those of you who have been coming on Monday and Tuesday evenings will have seen that this house is really becoming much too small for us. And also it is a great blessing for us that we now begin the permanent foundation of our monastery with a new group of people who seek to live their life according to the wisdom of St Benedict.

Since we last met you we have also received three new oblates, one of whom is in British Columbia, and also Isabelle who spent a couple of weeks with us here during the summer. She lives in London and wrote me a very amusing letter on her return telling me that she had told a friend of hers in London that she had become an oblate, and the friend looked most alarmed thinking it was some obscure disease she had caught while she was in Canada!

I want to say a word to you this afternoon about the spirit of the Rule of St Benedict and a word to you about St Benedict himself. I think if you look at the type of leaders we have you can see one of either two types – a leader who is cast in the *heroic* mould, a leader who is always pointing the way forward to what is beyond; or you can have a leader who is a sort of *father figure*. And the father figure is quite different from the heroic leader because the father figure is always saying, 'Let me decide for you. Don't go too far in that direction in case you come into problems or harm or difficulty. I'll take the decisions.' And if you think of this in the secular field, in ancient times someone like Alexander was a real heroic figure, with his vision of empire and so forth. In more modern times someone like Franklin Roosevelt in the States was a heroic type of leader, whereas someone like General Eisenhower was probably much more of a father figure.

Now, St Benedict, I think, is in the heroic mould because his vision of the Christian life which he is writing about in his Rule is a vision of a life that is constantly expanding. The horizons are always opening and for him the reason for this is that the Christian life is an openness to the wonder and mystery of God. The mystery and wonder that is itself infinite. What makes the Rule of St Benedict such an inspiring document – and this is why it has lasted for fifteen hundred years – is that

although St Benedict propounds this wonderful vision of a
Christian life, he never takes his feet off the ground. He is
constantly practical. He is constantly aware that the monastery,
the monastic community which stands for the Christian community, is composed of people who have all sorts of human
failings and weaknesses.

I'll give you just a couple of examples: the basic principle of
the Rule is to treat everyone you meet as Christ. Reverence
all, he says, as you would reverence Christ. Now, having laid
that down as an inspiring general principle he then goes on to
say but let the monk, for example, have a special regard for
guests who come to the monastery. And as you will read in the
Rule, he says that guests are never wanting in the monastery.
Many of us have found quite a few guests who are wanting, I
suppose, but generally speaking St Benedict says guests never
are. There will always be guests in the monastery and they
have got to be received in a very special way. Then he talks of
the old – let the monk show a *special* regard for the old in the
community as well as those who come to the monastery. He
says that their time of life requires a special understanding.
And he makes the same provision for the young. When he lays
down quite strict rules about fasting and so forth during Lent,
he says that nothing in this provision is to apply to old people
or to children. They have got to be given very special consideration.

Similarly, and you have to imagine the monastic buildings
with the long cloisters and people walking quickly from one
place to another, coming late for Office or work, he says be
especially patient with the slow-moving. Imagine getting behind
some old monk who is shuffling along down the cloister. St
Benedict actually puts in that special category. It helps to make
the Rule that he has written an extraordinarily human document. Everywhere compassion and understanding of human
limitation and human weakness.

But if it is so, equally the Rule is totally clear-sighted in
proclaiming the vision of what Christian life is in the establishment of the Kingdom. So, for example, St Benedict includes
the tools of good works in Chapter Four of the Rule where
you will read, 'Let the monk prefer nothing to Christ'. This

has got to be the first thing in their life – that they understand the wonder of Christ's life, that we all are redeemed and that our salvation is accomplished in Christ. Can you imagine, if everyone of us in this room could really understand this fact, it is not just that our own lives would be transformed, but that we would find it impossible not to transform the lives of all those we encounter in our own pilgrimage.

So there is this double strand in the Rule of St Benedict of absolute commitment, wonderful clarity of what God has achieved in Christ and, at the same time, an understanding that this vision has to be seen and responded to by weak, fallible, human beings. Now that is where I think we find the importance of the Rule for all of us, for us monks who live our lives and vows by the Rule of St Benedict and for you as oblates who seek to live this vision as it applies to you in your own lives. St Benedict is not saying, for a moment, that the essence of what it means to be a monk is that you wear the habit or the monastic tonsure or that you go around with your eyes cast down and all the rest of it. What he is saying is that the essence of the life of a monk is to love Christ as you love your neighbour. That is the importance of the Rule for all of us. That that openness to the divine mystery is the basis of our daily lives. For those of you who are married, it is the daily ratification of your own love for one another in the love of Christ. It is the love you have, for example, for your children, ratified in the love of Christ.

Above all, what the monastic synthesis is about is living our life within the Christian mystery. When St Benedict tells us to revere everyone, what he is telling us in essence is to be aware of the mystery that another person is. Again, if only all of us here could live that truth or live out of that truth, we would be aware of the mystery that the *other person* is and so live with the reverence that that would involve. The word that St Benedict uses, *reverentia*, means, from its ultimate derivation, living out of the *truth* of that relationship. And the truth in St Benedict's understanding of life is that everyone is a temple of the Holy Spirit. Everyone is a tabernacle of the Most High. That is why we have to treat one another with such sensitivity, with such reverence, with such love.

It isn't always easy. When I was a novice at Ealing there was once a knock at the door and I went down and there was an old man there, a chap who was trying to walk into central London. It was pouring with rain and he said, 'Have you got a pair of shoes here you could give me? I've got about five more miles to walk. My shoes have given out.' I said, 'What size do you take?' He said, 'Nine.' I said, 'Mine will be no good to you. I take elevens.' I thought there must be someone around here who takes nines, so I walked around the monastery and, as sometimes happens in monasteries, everyone seemed to be out. Not a soul was in his room. I went into one room, belonging to a very holy old monk of about eighty. And there were four pairs of shoes there. One of them very old-looking and three fairly new. I thought, well this chap will never wear these out in the years that are left to him. So I picked up the oldest pair and took them down and handed them to the chap. He was delighted, tried them on and they fitted perfectly. He walked off into London. About an hour later it was as though an atomic bomb had hit the monastery. Our abbot at that time was the last abbot I knew who wore a monocle. He came down, looked at me and said, 'A terrible thing has happened, Brother John, a frightful thing has happened. Someone has stolen a pair of Father Dominic's shoes.' I said, 'Oh no they haven't. I just gave them away to a man at the door.' At which the monocle fell out of the abbot's eye and he said, 'My dear, we can't do this sort of thing, you know. No one would ever feel confident leaving their room if they came back and their shoes or clothes had been given away.'

Well, now, that is just the sort of situation provided for in the vision of St Benedict. What I think all of us have got to try constantly to keep in mind is that when we meet that chap at the door, for St Benedict he is Christ. He was a poor man, and as you will see in the Rule, St Benedict says to receive everyone who comes with honour but especially the poor because, he said, a rich man who comes will be given respect because of his position and so the poor must be received with special honour. We all have to constantly keep in our minds that there is a mysterious dimension in our lives if only we can *remember* it, if only we can be *mindful* about it. That is the genius of the Rule of St Benedict – showing us how to remain mindful. Benedict so sets up the day of the monk and the structure of the monk's life that we need never forget this. This is the essence of what we have to share with you.

This is what we want to communicate to you. When we give the new oblates a copy of the Rule of St Benedict, this is the doctrine we want to put before you. To understand the mystery out of which we live our lives. As St Paul puts it, 'That mystery is Christ within you.' Now, that is why prayer is integral to the doctrine of St Benedict. As you know our monastery here is founded for this specific end, to share our prayer with everyone who comes to our house. There are some monasteries that are set up to found schools and hospitals and all sorts of places of good works that are necessary. And basically speaking Benedictine monks have always been prepared to do whatever work is necessary for the Church. We don't have a specific work as some other orders do. We are prepared to do anything for the good of the Church as seen by the local bishops or the Pope. For example, very shortly after the death of St Benedict, St Gregory who was himself Pope and a Benedictine monk asked St Augustine to lead a group of monks to England to convert the English to Christianity. Monks have always been prepared to respond to whatever needs the Church has. We are here because the Archbishop of Montreal asked us to come to respond to a specific need, namely to share our life of prayer with the Church in Montreal, to be open and available to whoever comes to our house.

Now for St Benedict this life of prayer was absolutely essential for the achieving of the vision. As I say, St Benedict is a leader cast in a heroic mould. He is not doing all our thinking for us. He is saying, 'This is the road to head out on. And you will be led into things that I do not know about, that I cannot even foresee in any way but you must set out on this road.' The road that he tells us to set out on is the road of daily prayer. He recognized that we would forget, that we might start with the best intentions and that we might really try to see Christ in our brethren. But we only have to encounter someone who keeps treading on our foot or getting in our way, and we quickly forget this vision that Benedict has propounded.

And so he had the monks return regularly throughout their day to their prayer.

That is why we urge you as sincerely as we can to root your lives in prayer too. To have your morning prayer, the prayer that you will find in the Breviary, psalms and readings and then your morning meditation where you can be silently aware of the power of Christ in your own hearts. And then to return to it again in the evening and to offer that evening prayer, psalms and readings from the New Testament, and then your evening meditation; this is to live again out of the same power, the power that is Christ.

One thing about the Rule that is perhaps unique to the Rule of St Benedict is that although the demand of the Rule is humanely presented, for St Benedict there is no half measure. For St Benedict you are either on the pilgrimage or not. There is no half measure in the Rule. Nevertheless, the essential quality of the Rule is the gentleness of St Benedict. I would like to end today by urging you in your lives as oblates to be gentle with yourselves. As you read the Rule and as you see the great vision that St Benedict propounds, you will encounter your own weakness, your own forgetfulness, your own stupidity. I suppose the most difficult thing any of us find to put up with is our own stupidity. Don't be disheartened, because what St Benedict constantly urges us to do is to begin, to start again.

For example, one of the things that he speaks of which is very practical and very basically Christian, is not to allow the sun to go down on your anger. If you are angry, if you have a grudge against someone, if there is any lack of forgiveness in your heart, try to exorcize that before the sun goes down. Don't let the sun go down on your anger. It is the gentleness of the Rule that I think is perhaps its most important characteristic for you as oblates. To understand that your lives can be transformed in the power of Christ. If you determine to the best of your ability to live out of his power, out of his love, then your lives can be transformed. But because it is the power of love that power is always a gentle type of way. It is one that is taking us relentlessly forward into the mystery of God. But with infinite gentleness, with infinite tenderness.

Now I just want to remind the new oblates again of the basic structure of the daily life of an oblate. What we urge you to do is, in so far as you can – be very human, be very gentle about this – to begin your day with morning prayer, and then your morning meditation. End the day with evening prayer and your evening meditation. During the day read a little excerpt from the Rule of St Benedict. We will give you a copy of the Rule and there is a short passage of the Rule that has the date of every day of the year on it. Read that short passage and then see in that passage what this means to you in your life. Very often you may find when you first read the Rule that there is very little that may be directly relevant to your life. But the more you read the Rule the more you will learn to get behind the particular dispositions to the spirit of what St Benedict is talking about. It is that spirit of St Benedict that has had such an enduring influence on world culture since the sixth century. Then, also, each day we would urge you to try to read something from the Bible, particularly from the New Testament. The Community and the Scriptures are the great sources of strength for our pilgrimage.

The Tranquil Pursuit

This afternoon we are going to receive six new oblate novices
– Don is from Ottawa and is hoping to start a meditation group
there; Tom who has been living with us in the community for
some months; Jim from New York who is also hoping to start
a group there; Agnes from England, who is making her second
visit to us and is hoping to start a group in Oxford; Hélène,
who has been coming to our groups here in Montreal for some
time, is from Montreal; and Jean who is a student, also from
Montreal, who has been coming to meditate with us for some
months now.

The Rule of St Benedict which is our common inspiration
has probably been printed, translated and commented upon
almost as much as the Bible itself. I suppose before the inven-
tion of printing it was one of the most copied manuscripts there
was. This is a rather astonishing fact because the Rule is written
for a very particular situation in mind – the establishment of a
monastery, the government of a monastery. Yet its wisdom has
struck men and women in every generation and walk of life.
Perhaps the reason is that St Benedict so perfectly struck the
note for this *particular* society that he struck a universal note.
And indeed the Rule is rather like the Gospels, in that it does
seem to have the capacity to reach people at whatever stage of
life they are at, or in whatever vocation they follow.

Today I want to talk about one particular aspect of the Rule.
That is its balance. St Benedict is quite clear in his mind that
the most important aim in life of the monk is to seek God.
And he doesn't compromise on that. Indeed the great note of
the Rule is its refusal to compromise. St Benedict's concept of
obedience, like his concept of the simplicity of the life of the
monk, are absolutely clear and demanding. They are so because

53

he wants the monk to understand the importance of seeking God. But he is a great human being. St Benedict is a man with a most loving heart and he understands the infirmity, the weakness of our will and of our flesh and so constantly in the Rule he lays down the principle: This is the way, but we want to encourage people to follow this way. And so let us not frighten them. Let us not discourage them. But rather let us encourage them.

Reflect on this from Chapter 34 of the Rule. The title is 'Distribution of goods according to need'.

> As it is written, distribution was made to every one according as he had need. Therefore we say that in the monastery there should be no favouritism – God forbid – but let there always be consideration for infirmities.

What St Benedict is saying is, let everyone in the monastery be treated in the same way, except those who need more or who need special consideration. He goes on,

> Let the monk who has need of less, give thanks to God and not be grieved and let the monk who requires more be humble because of his need.

I think there you have the principle that you can apply to every part of life. What we have to try to do is to serve God with the greatest generosity possible. What we have to do in our relationships with others is to help them to serve God with the greatest generosity possible for them.

Now the important thing to understand – and this is threatened by the weakness that we have to be always on our guard against – is that the searching for God must burn at the purest possible level in our hearts. St Benedict urges us, as regards ourselves, not to be discouraged if we can't always achieve the purity of intention that we would like to achieve but to be humble when we achieve less. We must understand that all the achieving is in the gift of God. As regards others, let us never judge others harshly. Remember the words, 'let there be consideration for infirmity'. If we judge ourselves and discover that we have to be humble then we must bring that humility to our relationships with others. Now each of you will discover how this principle applies in your own life, in the relationships with your friends or within your families. The example that each of us has to give is to strive for the realization of the Kingdom of Heaven, the Kingdom of God, the Kingdom of love and peace, and to strive for it with all the generosity and all the energy that we possess.

But when we don't achieve everything we would like to achieve, and so often our ideals outstrip our capacity for generosity, we must be humble and, avoiding self-rejection turn to God and seek new strength, new encouragement in him. In our relationships with others the greatest teacher is example. 'Let him that has need of less give thanks to God.' What St Benedict suggests here is that the cheerfulness of our own giving and generosity, our simplicity, our single-mindedness in seeking God, is the best way we have of proclaiming the Kingdom. Much more powerful than words, much more powerful than criticism of others is our own example. And in all our relationships with others always to follow the rule of gentleness and encouragement.

Then he gives us a very wise piece of advice. He says, telling the monk who requires more, 'let him be humble because of his infirmity and let him not be made proud by the kindness shown to him'. So in his vision we avoid becoming proud or demanding. The result of this attitude held in common he sees like this: 'and thus all the members of God's family shall be at peace'.

Here you have the essence of the Rule – to strive for God and to make your spiritual journey the underpinning reality of your life, finding its influence in everything you do, in everything you are. And if you do, the result is peace. Peace in your heart. The monk is above all a man of peace. You as oblates have this great gift to bring to your family and into your lives, this gift of peace. The peace that Jesus tells us is beyond all understanding.

It is a peace that is the harmony of order. The Rule of St Benedict for the monastery has as its aim to create a society where there is harmony and order so that the seeking of God may go forward untroubled and unhindered. And so each of us in our own hearts must try to establish that same harmony and order, that same tranquillity and peace for exactly this reason, so that in all our hearts there may be that same tranquil pursuit of God and so that all our lives become truly Godly.

We all know that when we start our pilgrimage all sorts of powerful forces are pulling us one way or the other. St Benedict tells us to be humble about this, to be patient with ourselves. He tells us to be humble because our pilgrimage must be a *real* pilgrimage. It is the *real* you and the *real* me who are on this journey and the genius of the Rule of St Benedict is that it is not written for angels. It is not written for disembodied spirits but for weak human beings, human beings who bear within themselves all the faults, all the weaknesses of an enfleshed existence. The genius of St Benedict is that taking very ordinary material, he puts it forward as a perfectly realizable aim. It is to move gradually and gently with the teaching of the tradition of the monastery and the encouragement of the brethren towards greater generosity, greater self-discipline, greater love. Listen to how St Benedict ends his Prologue to the Rule when he tells us that the final aim of the monk is seeking to serve the Lord with joy, to follow Christ with faith.

Our aim then is to establish a school of the Lord's service and in setting up this school we hope to ordain nothing that is either harsh or rigorous. But if anything be somewhat strictly laid down because right reason demands it for the amendment of vice or the preservation of charity, do not at once be dismayed and seek to leave the way of salvation. (*Remember beginning to follow the way of meditation must be difficult and demanding.*) But as we go forward in our life and in faith our hearts shall be made more generous and with indescribable love we will learn to run in the way of God's commandments. Learning this we will never depart from his guidance but will learn to persevere in his teaching in the monastery until death. And may we learn by patience to share in the sufferings of Christ so that we may deserve to be partakers in his Kingdom.

Consecrating Everything

This is from Chapter 43 of the Rule by St Benedict:

As soon as the signal for the Divine Office has been heard let the monks abandon what they have in hand and assemble with the greatest speed, yet soberly so that no occasion be given for levity. Let nothing be put before the work of God. If anyone arrive at the Night Office after the Gloria of the 94th Psalm which we wish, for this reason, to be said very slowly and deliberately, let him not take his proper place in the choir, but stand last of all, in a place apart which the abbot has appointed for careless persons so that they may be seen by him and by all until the completion of the work of God to which they must do penance by public satisfaction.

I read that to you because this is an example of a passage in the Rule which you might wonder if it has any application for you as an oblate of St Benedict. I read it too because over the past week I have been talking with Don and June, two of our oblates who have been making a month's retreat with us. One of the things we have talked about together is how they, as lay people, are to be expected to put so much of the text of the Rule into practice in their life when it seems to have so little application to their state of life.

As well as talking about these things I have been listening to some tapes that were sent to me. I couldn't get to the end of them. They were on spirituality and one of the recommendations of the good man who made the tapes was that things have got so bad in the Church that we have got to have courses on spirituality in all colleges and universities, dioceses and parishes. He says these haven't got to be just any courses on spirituality. They have got to be at least of PhD standard. It is extraordinary that people can put such things forward with such seriousness and, I suppose, sincerity.

Putting these two ideas together it struck me that the Rule of St Benedict is not in the first instance about spirituality at all. The Rule is a highly practical document. There is no great theory that is proclaimed or put forward. It is a very practical document about ordinary living. The very practical spirit of St Benedict was due to the fact that he knew so clearly what monks were like – and I suppose what oblates are like. He knew they were likely to be gossips. This chapter goes on to stipulate that if they are late, don't let them stay outside the door because they are likely to gossip with one another. Let them come in and stand where they can be seen so that they won't either give way to gossip which would be very harmful to their souls or create a row outside laughing at the failings of the other monks who are in there singing the Office. So he understood very clearly about human nature, its sublime and ridiculous sides. I think he understood something that we have to be very sensitive about, what religious people are like.

He understood their limitations and their failings. When it is time for the Divine Office, for example, he says, 'let them drop what they have in hand and assemble with the greatest speed'. Now monks are extraordinarily compulsive people. I have found in my experience they get the most amazing compulsions. I know one monk, for example, who got a terrific fixation about weaving. Not weaving cloth, but basket work and the devil himself could hardly get him out of his weaving shop. He would say, 'I can't come! I am half way through this very delicate thing. This chair will be ruined if I stop . . . . ' It didn't matter whether all the signals for the Divine Office in the world had gone off at once, he couldn't be persuaded to leave.

Yet what St Benedict is saying to us throughout the Rule is that it isn't the great religious gestures that matter. So many of us are prepared to die for God as martyrs. We imagine colossal dramatic scenes where we make our final speech from the dock or to the firing squad. I suppose, depending on our temperament, we are prepared for that. But what St Benedict asks of us is something much more demanding. That is just to

58

live our everyday life with simple fidelity. When it comes to the time of our prayer or meditation or the Divine Office, we drop what we are doing and we go to it, simply. Furthermore, he says, go to it soberly, *cum gravitate*, seriously.

I think that is what religious people do need to understand. They need to be serious. Not solemn. Not seeing the thing as though abandoning what we are doing, because we love God so much, is a great act of service. But just because we understand that the worship of God and seeking to live on the bedrock of reality, which is God, is simply of the most supreme importance and not to do it would be stupidity. Indeed not to do it, as we heard in the Gospel of today's Mass, not to do it leads to *ruin*. That is the word Jesus uses.

Benedict asks this question of those who would follow his visions of life, of religion, of reality: *Do we really seek God?* That is why he says also in this chapter, 'Let nothing be put before the work of God.' You would think that is a strange sentence to put in a Rule for monks. After all, why would a person become a monk except that he should seek God? Yet it is so easy for all of us, particularly for religious people, to become bamboozled, sidetracked by the structures of life and above all by the structures of our religious life.

As I am sure I have said to most of you before, I think that it is a grave mistake to read too many books on prayer or on the spiritual life. Not just because so many of them seem to contain such extraordinary statements like the one about PhD spirituality, but because time is so precious. It is much better (and we learn this more and more) to spend our time in meditation than reading someone who is writing about someone else's writing of what it is like to pray. For St Benedict, the call is not to be a great expert on all the latest paperbacks on spirituality. The call is to simple fidelity. 'Let nothing be put before the work of God.' Even the theory of the work of God. Why should he have his priorities so clear? I think the reason is that he understands human nature so well. In the Gospel of today's Mass Jesus tells us that if we want to find our true selves, that is, to make deep real contact with the ground of our own being, then the thing to do is to take up our cross and follow him. St Benedict's Rule is a mirror of the Gospel and he knows perfectly well that if we do attempt to go for self-fulfilment, self-advancement, self-perfection the only result can be *ruin*.

As you read the Rule of St Benedict I think you will see more and more that the vision he proposes is a difficult one for people of our age and generation. The reason is that his doctrine flies in the face of conventional wisdom. Does the person who comes to be a monk really seek God? The conventional wisdom urges all of us to go for self-fulfilment, self-understanding, self-analysis. Even among Christians the cross is not spoken of in any very clear terms today. Yet if we do not tread that way and tread it faithfully there is nothing ahead but ruin. What we have to understand, those of us who try to follow the vision proclaimed by St Benedict, by our way of meditation, is that our meditation is not there for our own self-perfection. We are not seeking to become spiritual experts. We are not seeking to become spiritual teachers. We are only seeking to be available to God, to be available to him in our prayer, in our reflection upon the Word of God in Scripture, in our work and to have all this bound together by Divine Love.

If any of us wants to ask the question, 'How am I progressing in my life as a Benedictine oblate, as a Benedictine monk? Am I making progress?', don't look at your meditation. Don't look at your capacity for levitation. Don't judge your progress by the number of bumps on your head from hitting the ceiling. There is only one way we can judge our progress and that is by the quality of our love. By the quality of the love that we bring to our relationships. That is the marvel of the practicality of the Rule. St Benedict urges us to show honour to all. That is the test.

So to summarize, what I would like to make as clear as I can to you today is that the Rule and our daily reading of the Rule serves to bring us to understand that all the details, the humble, practical details of our everyday, are there to bring us into the mystery of Divine Love. Everything we do has that capacity if we enter into every moment with faith in the presence of God's love made real, made incarnate in our own hearts. St Benedict in the Rule asks us to remember constantly the Divine Presence, and his structure of the monastic day is designed to have us live every moment out of a vital sense of the Divine Presence in our midst and in our hearts. Now what I suggest to you as oblates of our community is that you share with us your commitment to meditation and to the search for God in your own hearts. According to the circumstances of your life individually, what we suggest to you is that you start every day by meditating in the morning so that you come to your day with a sense of that Presence of Christ in your heart as a reality. Then, that you return to your meditation in the evening. By returning in the evening you, as it were, bring every part of your day together and again offer it to God, consecrate it to him.

As oblates that is what you commit yourself to. To consecrate your life and to make sacred every part of it by being wholly alive to everything you do throughout the day. Our morning meditation, as it were, prepares us and strengthens us for the day and our evening meditation gathers it together and offers everything, the successes, failures, disappointments and the joys. Everything in your day is brought together and offered to God in the healing love of Christ. For those of you who are going to begin your life as oblates today, I would like to say this – understand that this is an ordinary way and a simple way. Perhaps the Rule could well be described as a document that shows us how to bring an unaccountable zeal to bear on things of no account, the small details of every day, just lived with faith and love. The vision of our community that we want to share with you is simply that the greatest need that the Church and the world has today is for men and women of integrity, men and women who are made whole by being wholly committed to the vision proclaimed by Jesus and who are open to his love established in our hearts. St Benedict is our guide because he sets out a way that is eminently practical, eminently wise and eminently human. That way is the way of faith, of trust in God and of absolute confidence in his power.

Obedience

If you want to understand what Jesus was preaching, then the best chance you have of understanding it is to come into contact with someone who is living his message. That's the essence, I think, of the communication of the gospel. I think a Christian monastery is simply a place where a group of Christians try to live that message, try to live the gospel. There's nothing very dramatic about it. It's just the simple fidelity to the ordinary things of every day. The essence of the proclamation of Jesus is that God is love. And in the monastery the basic rule of our life is that we try to love one another and we try to love everyone who comes to our monastery.

Your part in our monastery is a very important one because every Benedictine monastery has a particular character and the particular character of our monastery is that we want to try to communicate our message of meditation as widely as we can. Basically, what we're trying to communicate is the message that Jesus lives, that he is risen from the dead and that he lives in our hearts and that the invitation we all have is to make that pilgrimage to our heart, to be with him, to uncover his power within us. All of us begin wounded. All of us begin with our handicaps but our wounds and handicaps are nothing in the confrontation with that power of the love of Jesus in our hearts.

Now that is our message from this monastery and you, as oblates, are associated with us in communicating that message. And how is it communicated? By living the life of prayer, each of us, personally, by our own commitment. It isn't communicated in the first instance by speaking about it, by writing about it, by discussing it, by reading books about it. It's communicated by living it. As you know, our message is a very, very simple one – 'Say your mantra, every morning and every evening.' If we can live that, then we cannot help but communicate it. St Benedict's vision is of a society where the love of Jesus is supreme and is *the* supreme value. Whoever comes to the monastery must be received as we would receive Christ. We must see Christ in one another, we must see Christ in our abbot. Everywhere St Benedict calls us to seek for Christ, to find Christ and to worship Christ. Now, one of the questions that every oblate must ask themselves is, 'What has this Rule got to do with me as a layman or laywoman, as a married man or married woman, as a family man or as a professional man or woman – What has this monastic Rule got to do with me?' I am going to take one instance from the Rule to try to show you how important the Rule is in everyone's life because St Benedict, it's true, wrote his Rule for monks. But what he was writing was simply a distillation of the essence of Christian life and he then put into it an institutional framework to make it work in a community, in a monastery. But the underlying principles of it are universal.

Perhaps a thing that you don't see as obviously important for you is his doctrine of obedience. I suppose in the modern world obedience has been lost sight of as a value. When we think of obedience, we think immediately, I suppose, in terms of superior and inferior, of master and disciple. We think of it in those or similar terms. But for Benedict the whole of the monastic life is a growing in obedience. He says in the Prologue, 'Let us return to God by the path of obedience because we have strayed from that path by the sloth of disobedience.' And obedience here is in essence, sensitivity, deep sensitivity to the other, to the others. Everyone in their Christian life needs that sensitivity. The readiness to think, in the first place, of the other and not of oneself.

I had experience for some years in London as a marriage counsellor. I suppose it wouldn't be an exaggeration to say that one of the principle causes of the breakdown of so many marriages is a lack of the spirit of obedience. A lack that is equally the cause of the breakdown in the religious life where we lack a real sensitivity to one another, where we lack that determination to live, not out of our own egoism, but in the relationship of love. All the vows that we take in the monastery are concerned with right relationship. Obedience is a relationship that we have to one another, to the community, to the community at large, and within the monastery, to our abbot. The basis of the relationship is that we leave self behind. And we not only serve one another, we love one another. As you know, it is impossible for us to love one another unless we serve one another.

The genius of St Benedict was that he not only set out this vision of the Christian life in his Rule as a vision of selfless, generous love but he also set out the means whereby we may follow that vision. As you know, it is not good enough just to have the vision. It's necessary to set out on the road to enter that vision in reality. And St Benedict's genius was that he set up a framework, an institutional framework, wherein, if we are really faithful to it as monks, and if we ourselves are really committed to obedience, to selflessness, to proclaiming the gospel, rather than seeking our own comfort or convenience, then the result, he tells us in the Rule, is a life of indescribable joy. In St Benedict's understanding of it there should not be such a thing as a sad monk. The monk is one who by his degree of selflessness, his degree of service, his degree of loving relationship with the brethren is a free man. And in that freedom he experiences 'indescribable joy' as St Benedict puts it.

The key to it, or one of the principle keys to it, is obedience. The capacity to *listen* – to listen to the other, to listen to the Word, to listen to God. Everything in the Rule of St Benedict leads the monk forward to God. A monastery is not an end in itself. The Rule is not an end in itself. The habit is not an end in itself. Monastic life is not an end in itself. It leads the monk forward. Indeed, the Rule itself is self-transcending, as St Benedict sees the hermit life as lying beyond the monastery. Even beyond the hermitage there is Christ and beyond Christ there is the Father. Obedience is one of the essential qualities to achieve that vision and to realize it. *Obaudire* – the capacity to listen. We are perhaps at our most obedient when we meditate. That's the time when we are in our most selfless state. That is the time when we listen to the very heartbeat of creation itself. When we meditate our attention is wholly beyond ourselves. We transcend everything that we are and everything by which we know that we are. And we are obedient in God's presence.

I want to suggest to you that you reflect in your own lives as to how you can become more obedient, more sensitive, more open to the power of the Word, the Word spoken in your own heart, the Word that calls you beyond self into union with God. As oblates of our Community, sharing in our work, it's necessary for all of us, oblates and monks, to grow in this spirit of obedience because that is how we will communicate our message. The message that we have to communicate is one, I think, of great importance for the world, for the Church, for everyone – that a life that is not based on prayer, a Church that is not based on prayer, a world that is not based on prayer, cannot be a world, a Church or a life that is fully alive. The message that we have to communicate, and to try to do so as humbly and as faithfully as we can, is that the power of Jesus is *the* reality of time and history, the reality which everyone is invited to live out of and that it is the power of love. It's an astonishing thing that we, as a group, have been given the privilege, in our own small way, of trying to communicate this to people all over the world. What I want to urge each of you this afternoon is to be as faithful as you can be to entering as fully as you can into the essential life of your Community. And our essential life here are those times each day when we return to the fountain of life, to the living spring of water, to Christ, seeking him in our hearts as we meet to meditate four times every day.

Those of you who are making your oblation this afternoon are being given a special gift, a special grace. It's no small thing to have heard the message that Jesus lives. It's no small thing to try to base your life upon this message. And to do so within a tradition that has been alive in the world for centuries. Those of us who are monks, I think, always feel very humble and deeply grateful that we have somehow or other stumbled into this great tradition. Those of you who are making your oblation this afternoon are joining us in that tradition as fully as you can in your own lives. I want to urge you to read the Rule, to reflect upon it, and to see how the great wisdom of it can inspire you in your own lives to follow Christ more courageously, more faithfully and more lovingly.

All of us are called to establish the Kingdom of God and to establish it now. A kingdom that is without fear. It is a kingdom of love and peace. Our effectiveness in trying to turn back the tide of fear and hatred in the world depends upon our own insertion into the mystery of Christ. I want to urge you, above all, to be faithful to your daily meditation and to make that the rock on which you establish this pilgrimage. And so, make it the Way, the way you follow, leaving self behind and entering fully into the power of Christ's love. Everything else in your life flows from that. Your own worship as Christians, your own study and spiritual reading, everything flows from that personal encounter in your meditation because it's there that you find the power of love. It's there that you find your own conviction.

The Innocence of Christ

This afternoon I want to say a few words to you before we have the ceremony for those becoming full oblates. I want to talk to you about the sacredness of time.

One of the things about the monastic life is that it does seek to give each of us a sense of the sacred – a sense of God's presence – a sense of his purposes always being worked out, always being accomplished in the midst of our ordinary life. It might seem to you as oblates that this is more obvious in our life than it is in yours because with your life in the world you have to face the heat and the burden of so much more than we do in our privileged life. But I think in St Benedict's vision the monk is one who tries to find that sacred dimension in everything he does. I think exactly the same is true for you as oblates. In other words, there is really no such thing as anything that is purely secular if our heart is open to God's presence and to his purposes.

Part of that sacredness comes from the constant reflection upon the mystery of our Redemption in the liturgical year in the great seasons of Advent, Christmas, Lent, Easter, Pentecost – all those seasons we return to, constantly, deepening our understanding of the Christian mystery. Today I want to draw your attention to the season we are about to enter: Advent. Advent is the joyful preparation for Christmas. Christmas is the feast of great joy because our Redeemer comes. In all the great religious traditions, the Redeemer comes as a Child. He comes to restore to us our lost innocence, to restore us to a state of perfect childhood so that we are children of God, obedient to him, loving to him, anxious to serve him always as perfectly and as generously as we can. The monastic life has this very same quality to it. It is also a joyful preparation for the coming of the Redeemer. There is a real sense in which everyone of us who follow the way of St Benedict seek to find God, bring God forth from our hearts so that he is truly and personally born into our lives.

In the early monastic tradition the Fathers spoke of the end of monastic life being the Kingdom of God – that was its purpose. But the way they spoke of coming to this end was *purity of heart*. To come to the Kingdom, to the fullness of the Kingdom, we have to purify our own heart. That is what Advent is about. As we spend these next four weeks we must try to deepen our own purity of heart, to purify our hearts so that we are ready for the coming of the Redeemer, ready for his innocence. Ready to be open to his innocence and to be transformed by it. I think we can truly describe monastic life as a way of innocence. A monastery must be a place of joy, a place where we are children of the Light, free to be ourselves, free to live with our brethren in harmony. The harmony comes from our common openness to Christ, to our Redeemer and to our Redemption. The innocence brings with it liberty of spirit. That gives us the confidence with which we can approach one another. I think you as oblates share in that same sort of confidence, innocence and liberty. We see your association with our monastery as an enrichment for us. Our monastic life and our monastic ideal strikes a chord in your hearts revealing a new harmony, a new dimension.

For all of us, this is important because our purpose, the purpose of every one of us, monks and oblates, is to proclaim the Redeemer and his redemptive love to the whole world. We do so because we know him. That is really what monastic life is about – that we should know him, know him ever more perfectly and ever more profoundly. Everything in the monastery, everything in monastic life is directed towards that end, that we should know him and proclaim him. All our discipline, all our selflessness, all our silence, all our prayer, everything is directed to that one end, that we know him, and knowing him, we *must* proclaim him. The monastery must be a place of sacredness. It must be a place that constantly speaks to us who live here and all who come here of the Mystery within which we live. We must know the time of every day as shot through with his love, with the gift of his redemption. Whatever we are doing, whatever our work, whatever our task, we do it for him, with him, in him. We know him. We know him in our prayer, in our life of community and charity, in our service to one another and our dedication to his Kingdom.

For those who will make their oblation this afternoon, that is what they seek to do as oblates, to dedicate not just, as it were, the religious part of their lives, but the whole of their lives to Jesus, through him to God, and all in the power of the Holy Spirit. St Benedict's way is a way of gentleness. It is a way that is utterly single-minded.

All of us falter, all of us easily lose heart. The purpose of a Benedictine Community is, as St Benedict tells us, that we should encourage one another – and encourage one another gently. It takes all of us a long time to come to the perfection of obedience, to the perfection of chastity, to the perfection of poverty. But we do come to that perfection by the power of the love of that little Child whose feast we now prepare for. The monastic life and the vision of St Benedict is only possible because we believe that that Child is the Son of God. That Child comes to infuse each one of us with light and life. We would like to be able to share our monastic vision with the whole world but not everybody can understand it. It is a wonderful thing for us, as monks of this Community, that you, as oblates, can understand it. Your sharing of our understanding of that vision of St Benedict is very precious to us.

Listen to this from the Letter to the Corinthians. Here St Paul sets out the way of glory that we are summoned to as Christians. The glory that he speaks of, I think, is the glory of the innocence of Christ – a glory to which we are all summoned. Listen to this.

To this very day every time the Law of Moses is read, a veil lies over the mind of the hearers. However, as Scripture says of Moses, 'Whenever he turns to the Lord, the veil is removed.' Now 'the Lord' of whom this passage speaks is the Spirit; and where the Spirit of the Lord is, there is liberty. And because for us, there is no veil over the face, we all reflect, as in a mirror, the splendour of the Lord and thus we are transfigured into his likeness from splendour to splendour. Such is the influence of the Lord who is Spirit. (2 Cor. 3:12–18)

That is what the monastic life is about – transformation from splendour to splendour. All of this reflecting the splendour of the Lord.

The Benedictine Way

When we were starting some five years ago, I was in Montreal for the first time and a couple of the diocesan priests, after I had given a talk, took me aside and said, 'Now John, is this going to be a "one-man show"?' I said I supposed everything that starts starts as a 'one-man show' but fortunately when I went back to England, Father Laurence offered to come and so it became a two-man show. With the profession, I am happy to tell you, shortly of a third monk, Brother Paul, we really establish ourselves as a Community and we look forward soon to the profession of others.

One of the wonderful things about people coming to join us is that they come to a Community that had no prospects at all when they first came and when we were really just starting. It was a considerable act of faith on their part to leave everything, to leave their careers, to leave their families and to come on a very risky enterprise.

One of the beautiful things about the development of our Community has been the association we have had with you, our oblates, and it is a great happiness for us this afternoon that we are going to receive the Final Oblation of Andy who has been in touch with us now for over two years.

It is a wonderful thing for us that our life is enriched by our contact with you. Because we do not really want to be just another religious house. What we want to be is a community of people who are united by a reality that is greater than any of us. The purpose of our Community is to hand on the Christian tradition of meditation. What we are handing on, or trying to hand on, is the knowledge that Christ dwells in our hearts. That is a truth that none of us can contain in our puny minds and that none of us can ever adequately express. It is a truth

71

of staggering proportions. The wonderful thing is that it is a truth that contains us all. That is where we are united. That is where each of us, in our own way, whether we are monks or lay people, is devoted to the grand reality. Brother Paul, before he became a monk, was a lawyer. He spent years of preparation, studying the rules of equity and many other rules and suffered as he went a good deal of punishment trying to learn the corpus of the Civil Law. Now when he comes to us, we ask him to do the cooking. All his considerable intellectual attainments he puts aside to serve the Community, to serve Christ and to promote the ideal that we put forward of a life rooted and grounded in prayer. It is equally inspiring to us that so many of you, our oblates, come to us and give us such generous support and help enabling us to promote the Kingdom of God so much more effectively and so much more efficiently because of your help.

So, I want to talk to you this afternoon, in particular, about St Benedict's great concept of conversion. Because as Andy makes his oblation this afternoon, he is committing his life to turn to Christ. The great wisdom of the Rule of St Benedict is that it is a direct onslaught on egoism. The monk, in the vision of St Benedict, is a joyful man. He is a free man. He is not a man who is subject to constraint. He is not a slave. He is a free man whose source of freedom is Jesus Christ. The road to that freedom is the royal road of conversion, the turning from self-will, the turning from egoism to the will of God. God's will is love. That is the source of his joy. He knows that his inner-being springs out of that endless unfathomable spring of love which is the Divine Reality, which is God himself.

Now all of us need to be trained in this way of egolessness. It does not just happen by magic. It requires the full commitment of our humanity and that is only possible as a result of the humanity of Christ. It is possible to tread this way of conversion because Christ's human consciousness is open and available for all of us to unite our consciousness to his. The big problem in Christianity is to *believe* it. All of us can agree in theory that the way of the ego is the way to sadness, the way to division, the way to hatred. We all know that from our own experience. What we need to find is the faith that it is possible for us to follow in the steps of Christ, that it is really possible for us not to be concerned primarily about ourselves, our own development, our own happiness, our own amusement, not to be constantly measuring reality against our involvement in it. What we have to do is to open to the fullness of reality that is to be found in God in his will, in his love.

What I would say to Andy this afternoon as he makes his oblation is this: Base your life on that spirit of conversion. Everything follows from that. Turn to God. Be open to his infinite love. Respond to it. And everything else flows from that – what we should do, where we should go, everything flows from that deep spirit of conversion. It requires courage. It requires a truly virile spirit not to sink back into the easy options of egoism, not to be content just to get through our lives but to live our lives to the full with joy, with enthusiasm, and with a real sense of the fun of life flowing from that liberty.

In a real sense what St Benedict sets out in the Rule is a way for the monk to return to his own innocence. That is what each of us is invited to do. As I said, the particular work of our monastery is to communicate and to proclaim the wonderful tradition of monastic prayer as the way of selflessness. We have a tremendous grace and gift in the monastery that our times of prayer regularly recur and it doesn't matter whether we feel like it or whether we want to. What matters is that at the times of prayer we put everything, our own self-will, aside and enter into the Divine will. Indeed, in our meditation, we become the Divine will. We become one with God who is love and we are lost in his love. We become his love.

The real problem in life is to find something to believe in and to believe in it so passionately that you would lay down your life rather than deny it. The great grace that all of us have been given is to believe in Jesus Christ, to believe in his presence in our hearts and to believe that he invites such of us to enter into that presence. That is an extraordinary gift to have been given. We have to learn, because it is a gift of such staggering proportions, to respond to it gradually, gently. When we begin, we cannot fully understand the sheer magnificence and wonder of it. Each time we return to meditate we enter into that reality a little more deeply, a little more faithfully.

When we begin we probably find our way to meditation as one among many options that we have been looking at and it takes us time to find that this is the *pearl of great price*. This is the pearl that requires us to sell everything else so that we may pursue it with deepening purity of heart. That conversion that St Benedict speaks of is the dynamic reality, underlying everything in life. Turning from self to the other, to God and in that turning experiencing what St Benedict calls a joy that is utterly beyond description and that takes us absolutely beyond ourselves.

What I would say to you, Andy, is to remember that joyfulness, freedom, liberty of spirit – these are the hallmarks of the Benedictine life. A monastery can serve the world only, I think, in proportion to its own spirit of liberty, its own spirit of joy, its own spirit of delirium, arising from its knowledge that the Lord Jesus lives and lives in our hearts. The Benedictine Way, I think, transforms one's life by this joy.

A Self-Transcending Rule

We are living in a time of extraordinary change and the monastery like every other institution in our society is itself changing very rapidly. In the old days there was a steady stream of young men who came to monasteries who were easily capable, in the very stable society that they came from, of committing themselves to the monastery and to its work for life. Now in our society that pattern has changed quite radically and I think the numbers of monks in monasteries will decline quite rapidly in our time. Hopefully, we will be able to find here a small group of men who will be able to devote themselves full time, for life, to the single-minded pursuit of God. But it is unlikely, I think, that they will come in the future in great numbers.

Now in the way of the divine plan one door never closes without another door opening. I think that the oblate group attached to any monastery is going to assume an ever greater importance in the future. The oblate group will not just be a pious group who associate themselves externally with the monastery and, as it were, bask in its reflected glory. The oblate group, I think, from this moment on, will be a group who can undertake a real responsibility for communicating the vision of St Benedict. The oblate group will be a group of mature, committed Christians who can share whole-heartedly in the teaching function of the monastery and in its single-minded pursuit of God.

One of the great encouragements that we have as a monastery is the number of our oblates who have taken the initiative to establish groups to share with others the tradition of monastic prayer, of Christian meditation. It is a great joy for us today that Diane, who has established such a group, will be making her Final Oblation and Gerry who leads another group will be joining us as an oblate novice. This is a wonderful tribute to the vision of monasticism that is entirely contemporary.

Someone asked me the other day, who was considering becoming an oblate, what is the essence of the Rule of St Benedict. I think we can say that the essence of the Rule of St Benedict is that it is a document that in every chapter, every line, in every word, is self-transcending. St Benedict is constantly pointing ahead, beyond the monastery, beyond the Rule, beyond the institution of monasticism to God. His basic theme and constant message is that the purpose of everything we do in the monastery, the very purpose of the gift of our own life, is that we transcend self. To go beyond self is another way of saying that we go beyond all our own limitations and enter into the unlimited freedom of God. Listen to these words of his in the first Chapter of the Rule. He is talking about the various kinds of monks that there are – not good, bad and indifferent – but he is talking about cenobites, anchorites and sarabites. He says that:

> Secondly there are the hermits who have come through the test of living in a monastery for a long time and have passed beyond the first fervour of monastic life. Thanks to the help and guidance of many they are now trained to fight against the devil. They have built up their strength and go from the battle line in the ranks of their brothers to the single combat of the desert. Self-reliant now without the support of another, they are ready, with God's help, to grapple single-handed with the vices of body and mind.

I read that to you because it shows so clearly that St Benedict himself points beyond the monastery. The monastic life, in other words, is not an end in itself, just as the sacramental life or the celebration of the Eucharist as a sacrament is not an end in itself. It is there to point us beyond, to the infinity of God. And what is the essential quality that the monk needs in order to pursue this vision? Again, in the vision of St Benedict, the quality he or she requires is generosity.

Just consider the aspect, for example, of community living. Someone recently sent me the programme for a course on developing relationships or the skills for human relationships.

As I read the outline of this course it struck me that we have come to an astonishing pass in human relationships, now that we have to undertake a course in order to learn how not to tread on people's toes or the importance of passing them the salt at the table or whatever it might be. All these elementary human skills, it appears, and I am prepared to believe it, have become so buried, so lost, that we have to line up to pay our two thousand dollars and sign on for the course and hopefully learn to pass the salt or not to tread on people's toes.

Now if you look at the Rule of St Benedict, what does Benedict say about the essence of community living? The essence of community living for him is to find Christ in everyone. In other words, to find that hidden enlightenment in everyone. And St Benedict is no theoretician. He says we must find Christ in everyone, in the poor who come to the monastery, in the awkward; and sometimes it requires enormous patience to deal with some stubborn, awkward person in community. But St Benedict doesn't just tell us to tolerate, he doesn't just tell us to put up with them. What he says is, find Christ in them and finding him, worship him.

The difference I think between St Benedict and a modern programmer of one of these courses is that St Benedict does not ask us to look upon community or our religious development in terms of self-fulfilment but in terms of self-transcendence. The result is, if we really understand what self-transcendence is about, that we are constantly going beyond ourselves to the other. What that means is that we are constantly *meeting* the other. We are not engaged in any sort of search for our own fulfilment, looking for our own perfection. As he said, ask yourself not what is good for me but what is good for the other?

The monk who tries with all the generosity of his or her heart to live this understanding of life can never be lonely. He can never be isolated because the monk living this is always finding Jesus – in the abbot, in the brethren, in the sick, in the pilgrims who come to the monastery. Everywhere the monk who is leading the life put forth in the Rule is, as it were, saturated with Christ. As you know, Christ himself is constantly pointing beyond himself to the Father. So, everywhere the essential message of the Rule is self-transcendence. A group of brethren, however limited they may be personally, whatever their faults, and monks do not set aside their faults by putting on the habit, living this vision, with all the generosity of which they are capable, cannot help but be a group who are saturated with the Spirit of Christ. Our oblate group is a group invited to share this vision, to live this vision and to share this vision with others.

This afternoon we are going to receive two new oblate novices and we are going to receive two other oblates into our family as they make their Final Oblation. What we are doing is sharing with them the vision of this great spirit of St Benedict who points beyond himself to God. His message to us is support one another, encourage one another and in this fraternity of encouragement and support find Christ in one another. And having found him, proclaim him to all the world. That's why this afternoon is an occasion of such happiness and joy to us and for us who are monks, the reason for our joy is that we have found brethren with whom we can share this vision, this ideal and, above all, this *reality*.

Fellow-Pilgrims with Christ

I am sorry if we are somewhat delayed in starting. It seems that some special arrangements had to be taken care of. (*A surprise celebration of the fifth anniversary of our arrival in Montreal organized by oblates.*)

In the Prologue St Benedict tells us that the monastic life, the Christian life, is about opening our eyes to the divinizing light. Our pilgrimage of meditation teaches us that this light comes to us like the narrowness of a beam of light that is more and more concentrated. And although it is so narrow it leads into the wide and glorious vision of God and because it does so it leads to a wide and glorious vision of each other. And there we discover ourselves as possessing unexpected capacities for generosity, for forgiveness, for compassion. But we have no idea until then of what we do possess. We could not imagine that we could possess anything in such abundance. And that breadth of vision comes from our fidelity to the narrowness of attention. And our attention narrows down to the one word.

I think what we have experienced in our own monastery in our own small way is that where this narrowness of attention and fidelity to the practice flourishes, so does generosity flourish, so does love flourish, so does forgiveness flourish. And it is a life of *such* generosity. What is the explanation of this? Why should there be such a breadth of vision arising from such narrowness of discipline?

I think St Benedict, in the Rule, gives us the answer with his usual crystal clarity. The answer is to be found in one word – Christ. Because the purpose of our search, the end of our discipline, the whole *raison d'être* of our practice is Jesus Christ. That we may be one with him. Life is full of suffering. Life is full of pain. But none of that suffering or pain has any ultimate power over us or any ultimate significance for us when compared to the sufferings and pain of Christ. For in his sufferings we are made whole.

St Benedict tells us to seek Christ everywhere and in everyone. Above all in the guests that come to the monastery. Let them be received as we would receive Christ. All monasteries I suppose have jokes about the kind of guests, problem-people that they encounter over the years. But if they have, I think every monastery knows too that in its reception of guests there is still a very great grace. Often guests don't perhaps understand the fullness of the way of the monastery. They don't understand our meditation or they don't understand the absoluteness of our commitment to it. But that must in no way inhibit our searching for Christ in the guest.

Today I want to put very clearly before you the specifically Christian element in our search. We search for God through Christ, in Christ and with Christ. We are fellow-pilgrims with him. Now the essence of the Rule of St Benedict is that it is a Rule that holds this very clear reality before our eyes on every page. We must seek Christ in the young, in the sick, in the old, in those of awkward temperament, in those who are slow-moving, in the abbot, in the guests who come to the monastery. Everywhere we live our life is surrounded by this Christic dimension of love. Seeking Christ means that we open our consciousness to his. We begin to see with his vision, to love with his heart, and to do so without counting the cost.

When we receive our new oblate novices this afternoon we are not just going through some sort of legal rite or some form of merely outward ceremonial. What we seek to do is to contain within a short ceremony a reality. And the reality that we share with our oblates is this vision of Christ. We share with them this vision of understanding his unique mission to the world and of understanding too that since his life, death and resurrection the possibilities of human consciousness have been utterly transformed. It is possible now for us to enter into the presence of God through the human consciousness of Christ.

We urge each of our oblates to spend a period each morning and another each evening in meditation. The purpose of that pilgrimage one turns to each morning and each evening is simply to deepen this consciousness of Christ in our hearts, in our midst and in our brotherhood. We are all of us weak. We would, all of us, like to be more faithful, more truthful, more courageous, more loving. Yet we know there is still room for development on all those fronts. And it is in the Community that we find the opportunity for strength to become more truthful, to become more loyal to an ideal that is infinitely greater than ourselves. That ideal is nothing less than the Kingdom of God. A monastery is a microcosm of the Kingdom. The Kingdom is courtesy, is love, it is law, it is peace.

Today is a very happy day for us in the monastery and we are aware that happiness arises in our heart because of your love. The love, the thoughtfulness of our oblates. As we receive our new novices now let us be truly grateful to God that he has given us one another. It is not always easy to find a person to share with. What is a great grace to us is that we have found one another. And what we share is Christ, his love for us, his love for the Father. In that sharing we become, not just fully Benedictine, not just fully Christian, but fully human, fully the persons we were created to be.

Detail and Vision

In case I get carried away at the end and forget to give you the news items, we will start with the news. First of all I would like to say a word of welcome to Dame Gertrude. Dame Gertrude is a nun of Stanbrook Abbey in England, one of the oldest monastic foundations for women in the world and she is over in the United States giving a hand to a new convent that is starting at Still River. She has been able to spare some time to come and visit us so we would like to welcome her and hope that you will have a chance to meet her at tea afterwards . . .

One of the marks of the greatness of the Rule is that it gives the reader the capacity to see the importance of the details of life while at the same time holding before our minds the vision of an entire life based on love of Christ and service of Christ, love of our brethren and service of our brethren. I suppose all of us, when we read the details of St Benedict's prescriptions for the recitation of Divine Office, begin to experience a certain tedium. He seems to go on and on about this psalm and that psalm, so many small points, so many precise instructions for the recitation of this particular psalm at this particular time. Yet then you consider that the overall plan is one of infinite care to legislate adequately for this very, very important part of the monk's life, the common worship of God in our vocal prayer together. Although the detail of the recitation of the Psalms can make us feel a certain tedium, nevertheless when we look at the provisions on the whole canvas we see a wonderful care for one of the principal parts of the monastic life.

Indeed, unless we do approach the Divine Office with an eye to detail we will begin to lose sight of the essential purpose of our coming together, namely that we do worship God in our lives as monks in a continuous round of common prayer. The

Rule is, I think, like a vast canvas that has a really detailed foreground and an inspiring background that sets off the entire vision of beauty. And we have to see that this is so in our lives, too. We don't just have some sort of vague general vision but the day to day details are all aligned on Christ, all contributing to the entire vision of beauty. The purpose of our life is that we should give glory to God, we should enter into the real beauty of his Being and that there should be nothing ugly, there should be nothing that is not glorious in our lives.

Take another example – the weekly kitchen service. St Benedict legislates there in the most practical way right down to the last details, that the cloths that the servers have been using should be laundered and returned in a spic and span condition to the servers who are coming in for the following week. In other words, what he is showing in the Rule is that love for the brethren is no mere shallow matter. It is not just vague ideas about, 'Wouldn't it be nice if . . . ?' It is a highly practical thing that expresses itself in the most practical ways and the kitchen service, for example, shows the most practical ways of cleanliness, of thoughtfulness, of charity, true charity.

And so it's no good just making protestations about community living and community loving. It is necessary to incarnate these concerns in the most common-sensical and practical ways possible. It is one of the great strengths of the Rule that it is highly practical, highly common-sensical. I think for our oblates the same principles apply. It is no good, for example, meditating twice a day or saying the Office together or any sort of practice of this kind and it is no good having our 'spiritual' life in order unless our practical life is equally in order and commensurate with it. St Benedict would have us, in our lives as oblates, use the most practical ways to bring the high spiritual ideal that we seek to live into practice in our lives whether where we work, in our families or with our relations, in all our relationships.

St Benedict is no less eloquent when dealing with the vast vision of life, too. It would be wrong for us to be bogged down in detail so that we could see nothing but detail. And in the Prologue of the Rule, for example, St Benedict holds before us the great purpose of the monastic life:

Therefore, we intend to establish a school for the Lord's service . . . and as we progress in this life and in faith we shall run on the path of the Lord's commands, our hearts overflowing with the inexpressible delight of love.

And here is the great vision of the life. That if we can put the details in order, if we can be really practical in our love for one another, then our hearts really do expand. There is a real sense in which we learn to forgive. There is a real sense in which we learn to understand one another.

One of the most marvellous things I ever heard about a monastery was in one of our monasteries in England where one of the monks had committed a rather grave indiscretion. Someone came to one of his brethren and began to criticize him in a sneering sort of way. And he simply said, 'I don't want to hear what you are saying. You're talking about one of my brethren.'

I think that is what monastic life leads us to. We recognize that we are human beings with failings. We recognize that we are mortal. We recognize all our own human weaknesses and yet we recognize too that if we try to bring all that humanity and put it to the service of God then we enter on a way of life that does lead to expansion of heart and of vision. It is a vision that is truly Christlike and that calls us to greater and greater generosity, in learning, for example, to forgive ourselves, to understand ourselves. And certainly it leads to a greater generosity to love our brethren, to understand them and to love all those with whom we live and with whom we work. The world is in need of men and women who will be selfless and who will be understanding. And in St Benedict's vision of life there is always this clear memory that the great vision cannot be attained without commitment to small daily fidelities.

I want to read you in its entirety that little section from the Prologue:

Therefore we intend to establish a school of the Lord's service. In drawing its regulations we hope to set down nothing harsh, nothing burdensome. The good of all concerned, however, may prompt us to a little strictness in order to amend faults and to safeguard love. Do not be daunted immediately by fear and run away from the road that leads to salvation. It is bound to be narrow at the outset. But as we progress in the way of life and in faith we shall run on the path of God's commandments, our hearts overflowing with the inexpressible delight of love, never swerving from his instructions then but faithfully observing his teaching in the monastery until death, we shall through patience in the sufferings of Christ, deserve to share also in his Kingdom. Amen.

Now that is the vision that St Benedict puts before us. It is a vision of patience. It is a vision of love. It is one that calls each of us to an infinite generosity. And the wonder of it is that we find generosity in the monastery in our prayer. It might be that when you look at the Rule you wonder, 'Could I ever live like that? Could I ever possibly be able to achieve those high standards of living?' I think what each of us, those that are in the monastery and those of us outside, must realize is that the power to achieve this vision is given to us in our prayer. That is where we learn to have the courage to continue on the path, as St Benedict says, 'never swerving' from the instructions of Christ but always continuing on the Way that is Christ, until death.

Monastic Prayer Today

Preface

Many years before he himself became a monk John Main used to speak with friends about starting a 'new kind of community' that would answer the deep need for fellowship, oneness in mind and heart, that all people, not just Religious, feel. After he had become a monk he would talk of his vision of the ideal community in the most practical terms. He called it a community of love.

Monastic or religious communities only rarely convince us that they are primarily dedicated to love. Exterior works or religious observance are usually more dominant. Yet the contemporary need to renew the religious life in Christianity could only be met, in the vision John Main came to, by placing the experience of the God who is love at the centre of that life.

The current temptation is to attempt this at the psychological level, which is like trying to build a house from the first floor up. John Main's clear sense was that a religious life develops real community only when its members are rooted in the deeper level, that of their spirit. There each experiences the love of God for themselves and in this way is empowered to love God and others in return.

This talk on monastic prayer, given in the early days of the Montreal foundation, is about the way modern people in search of real communion can root themselves in the Spirit where we are already all one. It shows the deep stability of John Main's Christian anthropology: the monastic experience and tradition is a model of the whole Christian life; past experience and future evolution are in harmony when the present moment of God, entered into in prayer, is given central place; and the monastic life, like the whole Christian life, is not about restricting but liberating the potential of each human being.

89

Community of Love

Ideal and practice are often never further apart than in community, in human relationships. John Main's unique gift as teacher was to reveal the ideal as attainable in practice. He taught that the foundation of the practice is prayer. His authority was love.

Laurence Freeman OSB

Monastic Prayer Today

If we are to approach any subject with 'clear heads and open hearts' as Cardinal Newman put it, we have to ensure that our model for thinking about it is an appropriate one. Prayer itself, of course, is not concerned with thinking, no more than love is, and the essential model for prayer *is* love – the inter-personal dynamic of selfless and wholehearted acceptance and reciprocity.

When St Paul said that the Christian is one who says with faith 'Jesus is Lord',[1] he does not mean that the Christian is just one who *says* or *thinks* it. If that were all that it involved then when we stopped thinking 'Jesus is Lord' he would no longer be Lord for us and we would be merely part-time pilgrims – which is to say no pilgrim at all, because a pilgrim is one who stays on the pilgrimage. The faith St Paul was talking about is a reality that involves our whole person – that is, a reality that is woven right into the fabric of our being. We must put on Christ. The Christian call to transcendence is a call to utter fullness of being. Our faith in the Lord Jesus is a reality present to us whether we are thinking about it or not.

The model of prayer that I want to talk about tonight is not a model of an intellectual kind. In our approach to prayer any model that involves only a part of our being will be misleading. Prayer is the experience of the fullness of God – our model then must be able to bear the infinity of God, and the very minimum requirement for this will be that everything we are be involved.

It is my experience that the greatest scourge that afflicts the Church today is the widespread alienation from its own rich

1. Rom. 10:9.

tradition and experience of prayer. Countless numbers of Christians with a real thirst for prayer are having to make do with manuals of prayer instead of being able to encounter the living tradition. The greatest sign of hope of our times is that in every part of the world Christians are becoming more aware that there is a great religious and spiritual heritage, that forms, as it were, our human point of departure on the pilgrimage, the stepping-stone that leads us forward from the egoism of self-encapsulation to the transcendent reality.

In this talk I want to put before you something of the monastic tradition of prayer, which is and has always been one of the central channels by which the personal Christian experience has been communicated and one which I think is of great contemporary importance for Christianity.

I would like to stress for you that the monastery is pre-eminently a human community of loving persons. The popular conception of the monastery may be different. There are those who think of monks as having renounced ordinary personal relationships in order to concentrate only on themselves and God. Whenever this has been the case it has produced sorry monks and a dismal God. The truly loving community envisaged by St Benedict with monks living their monastic pilgrimage with 'a delight of love that cannot be described'[2] is a very different conception.

Whenever monasticism has lost touch with its own roots of prayer it has become progressively more lifeless and arid. But in the marvellous economy of the redemptive mystery whenever this does happen it never totally extinguishes the miracle of the personal experience of God's power at work in his world. Lost or suppressed in one place it emerges elsewhere refreshed and strengthened. There seems to be a merciful spiritual law that determines that whenever a Christian centre loses its vitalizing contact with the tradition, it loses both its own vitality and its position as a *centre* in the Christian community at large: the consciousness of the Spirit that gives it its power is transferred and descends elsewhere 'as it wills'.[3] And this tells us

2. *Rule of St Benedict*, tr. Bolton (Ealing Abbey, 1970), Prol.
3. Jn. 3:8.

something essential about the tradition. It shows that the tradition is, above all, an experience rediscovered and re-communicated for individuals and generations. It shows also that its totality consists in its being truly a reciprocal experience involving the creative consciousness of human beings. The tradition is a living experience to the degree that it is conscious. To put it another way: the purpose of the creation of human life is realized only when God can love himself in those who have awakened to the mystery of their own beings created in the likeness of God.[4]

Monks, like all human beings, can fall from grace. Monasticism can become decadent and the monastery instead of being, in the language of the Vatican Council, a sign for the world, can become a counter-sign – what Eliot called a receipt for deceit. Those of us who are monks would be foolish not to recognize this. But that this is so must ultimately be due to the fact that the particular monk or monastery has lost contact with the living experience of prayer – what Jesus called praying 'in Spirit and in truth'.[5]

That the monastic tradition can be lost suggests that somewhere in the complex of religious, political, social and economic reasons that have contributed to the collapse a false model of prayer has been formed. People have thought of prayer as a 'dialectical relationship with God', a way of pleasing or appeasing him, or a way of keeping him in touch with what is going on on earth – or a way of accumulating merit. Whatever the mutation, the model that Jesus expressed as ' . . . so that the love thou hadst for me may be in them, and I may be in them'[6] – this model, somehow becomes revalued on a materialistic scale. Once this has happened the deformation continues and materialistic values creep in on every side. The only way to reverse the spiral is to locate and reform the true model of prayer.

I speak to you as a monk about the monastic way because monks are ordinary people like yourselves seeking to make the fullest response to God in their own lives. They are, of course,

4. cf. Saccidananda, *Abhishiktananda* (Delhi, ISPCK, 1974).
5. Jn. 4:24.
6. Jn. 17:26.

but one means of handing on the tradition. But the monastery does offer a very clear and direct witness of the essence of the Christian life that it follows. In the monastery priorities are arranged so that the essential elements of the fully Christian response stand out in clear relief. The monastery is important, too, because of its humanity. Like yourselves monks can go astray and lose contact with the vitality and inspiration of the gospel. In this sense the monastery is a microcosm of all society.

The essential model for prayer then is the model of love – transcendence in union. The basic requirement for love is that both persons should be conscious – that is to say, fully open and wholly turned towards the other. And this is why prayer, which I have spoken to you of as our openness to love at every level of our being, is also the means by which we become fully conscious: aware of our own personhood through our openness to the personal presence of the Spirit of Jesus at the centre of our being. Any truly 'personal' relationship is a pilgrimage and an exploration and a discovery: we discover ourselves no less than the other. The hitherto unknown reality of our true self emerges like a picture from a negative at the moment when we have immersed our whole self in the otherness of the one we love and turned wholly towards that person, not as a projection of our desire or need, but as they are in themselves.

If we want to understand prayer in its presentness to us we have to be able to draw the analogy between our human experience of love and our awareness of the love of God. In practice this analogy is not an intellectual concept at all: it is the real, daily context in which we become conscious of love itself as the central reality, the consciousness that *God is the centre*.

As we progress in prayer we find, in prayer itself, the harmonizing catalyst that keeps us always steady and free in our love of neighbour and our love of God. We are not moving from neighbour to God at all, of course. We are responding unselfconsciously to the infinite gift of liberty that the love of God bestows, that love 'in which we live and move and have our being'.[7] If it is love that is the centre of our consciousness

7. Acts 17:28.

and not the *I* – then all such misconceived distinctions fade away. It is just this unification of human life in the central experience of love that monasticism and the monastic tradition witness to. The exigencies of language still require the use of distinctions such as *higher* and *lower* levels of love but the experience of the tradition as recorded by witnesses like Aelred of Rievaulx testify to their transcendence:

> Was it not a foretaste of blessedness thus to love and be loved; thus to help and be helped; and in this way from the sweetness of fraternal charity to wing one's flight aloft to that more sublime splendour of divine love and, by the ladder of charity, now to mount to the embrace of Christ himself; and again to descend to the love of neighbour, there pleasantly to rest?[8]

Where the analogy of human love and prayer usually gets distorted and alienated from the tradition is when there is no real human experience of love to make the human side of the analogy authentic. Lacking this, Christianity talks of laws rather than of liberty, of duty rather than gift and opportunity; the ugliness of an inhuman Christianity is created by the tragedy of people who have never been made human, never become persons in the experience of being loved. We are only fully human if we are in touch with ourselves, linked to our own centre and this can only happen if we are verified and affirmed in our existence by the experience of love. The whole span of a human life is – or should be – an ever greater affirmation of our existence. We begin with the experience of our parents' love for us. That endows us with enough confidence to make friends of our own. Then we are led to develop the capacity for real, selfless love: for delighting in another person's existence. And that leads us into personal, intimate love from where we begin our pilgrimage to the fullness of our being which is the complete experience of love in its most personal form: the experience of God in Jesus. This is all a natural process of growth 'led by the Spirit'[9] which leads to the mature awareness

8. Aelred of Rievaulx, *Spiritual Friendship* (Cistercian Fathers Series 5), 3:127.
9. Gal. 5:18.

that everything proceeds from love, is held together and grows in love and returns with the realized gift of personal consciousness to love.

This is why the Christian involvement with what the gospel calls the 'poor' – those wounded by lovelessness – is so essential. Jesus taught the simple task of loving our neighbour because of the vital importance to each of us to have had the experience of being loved by another human being. As we are created as *human* beings this is the prerequisite for realizing our destiny of fulfilment in the love of God. This is why, too, the Christian life is inseparable from prayer and the degrees of silence and solitude to which prayer calls us – why the monastery and the market-place are so dynamically related.

Unless someone has had the experience of being loved they are wounded, unalive at the centre of their being where their awareness of God awakes to realize them as person and release their divine gift of loving others, of turning away from self. The monastery shares deeply in the responsibility of healing those who – more and more in our own society – have been wounded by this non-experience of love. But also the monastery is a place where in all simplicity and steadiness a living witness is being made to the human capacity for love, and the possibility of being transformed by the direct experience of the love of God – at the centre, in the heart of every person. It is a place, then, that testifies to the liberty of God to act as he will, to transcend the laws and conventions by which people have to limit the ordinary working of their lives and relationships. A monastery is a *centre of prayer* only to the degree that it is a community of love: the prayer is an openness to the love, the monastery is the communication of that love to all within it and to all who encounter it. It is above all a fully human society that goes beyond materialistic conventions only to be the more personal, the more human, and therefore to receive and share the inestimable gift of knowing the experience of being loved and so recognizing the power of love to heal and redeem. From this human experience a depth is opened up in people that is itself the depth of prayer. Confident in their own being because of the love of the brethren, a person can then leave themself behind and enter into that depth which opens onto the limitlessness of love as the basic energy of all being.

The monastery realizes this ideal by its fidelity to the tradition in which it is located and by the personal appropriation of the tradition in its own circumstances.[10] Like all traditions the monastic tradition comes down to us in books and through institutions but it does not live until it has been encountered as an incarnate reality – until, that is, it has been re-engendered in a personal communication. A monastery is above all the place where the teaching is communicated by persons to persons in a fully human relationship. There can be no other way to communicate the mystery of the Christian experience because that mystery is one of a person: the person of Jesus whose full personhood already involves and contains ours. Again, this can sound very abstract until you approach it from the model of your own experience of love: in your marriage, your family, your friendships. If you try to approach prayer by the model of love I have been suggesting without rooting it in your own experience of human love you will be dealing with shadows and phantoms. Prayer is concerned with the reality and actuality of persons.

He who does not love his brother whom he has seen, how can he love God whom he has not seen?[11]

The monastic community is one where this grounding truth of the Christian life is both understood and courageously accepted. In the vision of St Benedict there is no community where this courage is lacking:

This zeal therefore monks should practise with the most burning love so as 'to be the first in showing honour to each other'. Let them bear with the weaknesses, whether of body or of character, with the most tolerant patience. Let them vie with one another in showing mutual obedience. Let no one follow what he thinks is useful to himself but what is of

10. RSB, chs. 18 and 55.
11. 1 Jn. 4:20.

use to another. Let them cherish mutual love chastely as brothers.[12]

As always with such a vision it is only too easy to evade the demands it makes on us by admiring it as a utopian ideal. But the wonder of the monastic tradition is that this ideal can and does find human realization in practice.

The day before yesterday, as I was walking the round of the cloister of the monastery, the brethren were sitting around forming as it were a most loving crown . . . In that multitude I found no one whom I did not love and no one by whom, I felt sure, I was not loved. I was filled with such joy that it surpassed all the delights of the world. I felt indeed my spirit transfused into all and the affection of all to have passed into me, so that I could say with the Prophet: Behold how good and pleasant it is for brethren to dwell in unity.[13]

St Benedict called the monastery a 'school of the Lord's service'[14] and one of its essential qualities is its power to teach the tradition as a living experience. This means something quite different from study and learning although these too are part of a monastic life. In the monastic experience the communication of the tradition has always been effected by those St Benedict called the 'spiritual fathers',[15] of whom the abbot is the exemplar: men whose own experience of the pilgrimage allows them to serve as channels of love, encouragement and practical admonition to those whom the Rule calls 'beginners'.[16] In the early days of monasticism, as we shall see shortly, these teachers of prayer were the heart of a monastery, the magnet that drew a community together and held it in the fraternal love of a life of prayer. They did not pray vicariously *for* others or assume their responsibilities for them. On the contrary, they led others, by the simplicity and constancy of their *doctrina* and the example of their own fidelity, stability and perseverance

12. RSB, ch. 72.
13. Aelred of Rievaulx, op. cit., 3:82.
14. RSB Prol.
15. RSB, tr. McCann (London, Burns and Oates, 1952), chs. 4 and 46; cf. ch. 63n, p. 198.
16. RSB, ch. 73.

in prayer, to a fully personal realization of each individual. Now such a relationship is always a sensitive one, within the Rule but not bound by *rules*. The teaching was a free gift, freely received and freely obeyed: it could not be imposed by force or maintained by fear. It could not be advertised because the disciple found the teacher, the teacher did not seek for disciples. And the basis of the communication was the faith commitment of the individual monks for whom the pilgrimage was their first priority. The *communion* of a monastic community does not consist in rules, local customs or forms of activity but in the reality of this personal commitment by each monk to something beyond himself: to the pilgrimage, to love of the brethren.

If a monastery is truly *on the Way* like this, committed to the tradition and to the love by which it is incarnated, it becomes a kind of focal point of the mystery of God. Because the commitment is of a particular kind, disciplined, direct and simple, the love poured out in the heart of each monk breaks through into the community and brings all who come into contact with it into the essential Christian experience of transcendence. It shows, too, in an endless variety of ways the power of love to transform, redeem and renew. This focal point of divine life involves a concentration of personal resources but this does not lead to exclusiveness or isolation. The incarnation of God's love comes to a penetrating, influential focus precisely to allow the mystery to enter and expand the hearts of all whose way leads them into contact with that focal point. Like the movement of all love it is always expansive, magnanimous and universal. Rooted in the personal mystery of Jesus in each of its members, the monastery is filled with the power that casts out all fear.

I have talked at some length about the humanity of monasticism for a reason. This evening I want to try to locate the monastic tradition of prayer for you in the mainstream of our Christian tradition and then to suggest to you how this monastic experience is of especial importance for us as men and women of the twentieth century. But at first hearing this teaching can seem to us today – monks no less than anyone else – so demanding an ascesis that we recoil from it. The degree of selflessness it calls for can seem a negation of our humanity. But we cannot reject the tradition like this without alienating ourselves from ourselves, so intimately are we involved in the tradition. This is why it is so important, if you are seriously concerned to follow the pilgrimage, to see it in the terms of the model of love rooted in our own experience and to possess the encouragement and personal affirmation that a loving community can give.

Central to the Christian tradition as it is, the monastic tradition of prayer is rooted and founded in the Jewish religious experience of God. At the heart of the Jewish response to the mystery of God was a profound reverence for the name of Yahweh. The name was both the sign or representation of the presence of God and the very presence of his power and glory. To 'fear this awful and glorious name'[17] was the first step in wisdom:

> For all the peoples walk each in the name of its god but we will walk in the name of Yahweh our God.[18]

What distinguished the Jewish revelation from the religions of their middle-eastern neighbours was the efficacy of *this* name of Yahweh, just as we shall see in a minute the special identity of Jesus is revealed in the name by which he calls God his Father and just as the early Christians were characterized by the name they invoked. Throughout the Psalms the name of Yahweh is a refuge, a powerful aid and an object of worship.[19] And the prayer of the devout Jew was centred on the presence and living power of this name – a power that the prophets declared had to be recognized and turned to *in the heart* and not merely on the lips. Significantly, the Jewish tradition called a holy man of prayer *baal schem* – master of the name.

It was in this religious tradition that Jesus preached the Kingdom of God. He declared that he came 'in my Father's name'[20] testifying to his reverence for the living power of God contained in the revelation of his name. He attributed the

17. Dt. 28:58.
18. Mich. 4:5.
19. cf. Pss. 44:20, 69:30, 83:18, 113:3, etc.
20. Jn. 5:43.

power manifest in his ministry to this same source: 'the works that I do in my Father's name, they bear witness to me'.[21] We know, too, from the Gospels that Jesus devoutly followed the regular Jewish hours of prayer, day by day, with their repeated call on the name of the Lord. But the name which was most characteristically used by Jesus of his Father was the word *Abba*. This was the name which scandalized the Jews because of its implicit claim to an intimacy of a special kind with God as *his* Father. This word was one of such special importance for the New Testament writers – undoubtedly the *ipsissima vox* of Jesus as it was – that they retained it in Aramaic, translating it for their Greek readers as *ho pater*, Father. The word was clearly honoured in the earliest Christian tradition as the special name that Jesus used when calling upon his Father in the repetitive prayer of the Jewish tradition. As a word, it summed up the heart of Jesus' own experience in prayer as openness to his Father.[22]

To the post-resurrection Jews who had followed Jesus and who were progressively experiencing the full revelation of his power and true identity, it was natural that the name of Jesus himself should take the place of the ineffable name of Yahweh. Jesus was the visible expression and full self-disclosure of Yahweh, he was the Son of God, the Word of God who had revealed to mankind everything he had heard from his Father.[23] The Word, the name of Jesus would ever after be, as St Paul described it:

> the name which is above every name, that at the name of Jesus every knee should bow . . . and every tongue confess that Jesus Christ is Lord.[24]

Similarly for Luke in Acts there was 'no other name under heaven by which we may be saved'.[25] The name of Jesus was the source of all power and authority in the early Christian communities who called upon the name of the Lord within the

21. Jn. 10:25.
22. cf. J. Jeremias, *Abba: Jesus et son Père* (Paris, Editions du Seuil, 1972).
23. Jn. 15:15.
24. Phil. 2:9.
25. Acts 4:12.

tradition of their ancestors but now in intimate communion with the Lord through the gift of the Spirit: in that name they were baptized, by it they were healed and through it they offered worship to the Father.

The name of Jesus clearly occupied a deep and central place in the early Christians' experience of the Spirit, not merely at a theological level but at the level of their practice of prayer. It was the most natural name to call upon in order to be led into the full, personal experience of the power of the Kingdom established in their heart by the indwelling Spirit. The tradition of this practice becomes explicit most evidently in the Eastern Church from the early fifth century. But the way was well paved from the tradition of the very early Church. Origen, for example, wrote:

> Today still the name of Jesus pacifies troubled souls, reduces demons, heals sickness; its use infuses a kind of marvellous sweetness; it assures purity of manners; it implies humanity, generosity, solicitude.[26]

After the founding of the great monastery of St Catherine on Sinai in 527 the tradition of calling upon the name of Jesus – either as a single word or in a short phrase such as 'Lord Jesus have mercy on me' – was seen as an act of faith-filled selflessness, a turning away from self in obedience to the Lord's command to leave self behind. It was an act whereby the whole person was led into the state of prayer, of openness to the love of God as Jesus was open to his Father. And in the teaching of these early masters of prayer the essential doctrine is simply to take a sacred phrase, word, or name and to repeat this: above all, to remain faithful to this simple repetition that leads beyond thought and imagination and quite beyond all self-conscious reflection.[27] As Simeon the New Theologian taught, the secret of prayer is simply 'keeping guard over the heart . . . the rest you will learn with the help of God.'[28]

This simple, practical wisdom of the East moved westwards

26. Origen, *Contra Cel*, Bk 1. ch. 7.
27. cf. John Climacus, *Patrologia Graeca*, t. 88, col. 112C.
28. *Method of Prayer and Sacred Attention*; cf. Hausherr, *La Méthode d'Oraison hesychaste*.

in the monastic tradition, and entered Europe through the influence of John Cassian who was St Benedict's teacher of prayer. In his Ninth and Tenth *Conferences* Cassian gave to Western monasticism his teaching on prayer which he himself had learnt during his years of discipleship with the Desert Fathers. In order to move into 'pure prayer' he advises us to take a short verse or word and then to cling to the constant repetition of it 'ceaselessly revolving it in the heart, having got rid of all kinds of other thoughts'.[29] He calls this the way to that 'continual prayer' that answers St Paul's injunction to 'pray without ceasing'.[30] It is not difficult to see how immediately relevant this is to ourselves. At the beginning of this talk I said that the challenge to us today is to root our faith that Jesus is Lord at a level of our being where it will be an abiding reality independent of the shifting movements of the mind. This was precisely the challenge that Cassian had in view in recommending this form of 'continual prayer', which is nothing less than the constant awareness of the Spirit of God praying in our heart, an awareness that 'renews our mind', that gives us 'the mind of Christ'.[31]

Cassian was quite clear that he was only handing on a tradition – but a tradition he had not only inherited but also practised and so had made a living tradition. He wrote that this doctrine 'was delivered to us by a few of those who were left of the oldest Fathers'[32] and he regarded it of central importance for a full response to the call of Christ to self-transcendence. It faced and overcame the two greatest obstacles to answering this call – what he called the 'blasphemy'[33] of anthropomorphic prayer – that is, conceiving of God in images and then praying or talking to the image we have made – and of the distractedness and restlessness of the mind and heart – the continual flux of thought and feeling. In both these obstacles to prayer Cassian saw that self-preoccupation and self-centredness hold us back from the

29. *Conferences* X:10.
30. 1 Thess. 5:17.
31. 1 Cor. 2:16.
32. *Conf.* X:10.
33. *Conf.* X:1.

103

redemptive encounter with the Otherness of God in which we discover our true self.

Cassian's teaching is fully within the tradition of the teaching of Jesus 'not to go babbling on like the heathens do',[34] not to make of God a convenient shoulder to cry on and in our *talking things over with him* to lose sight of the wonder and otherness of his love – the essential mystery of his being. The power of his message consists in its utter simplicity. Unless you become childlike, Jesus had said, you will not enter into the Kingdom of Heaven. And Cassian's teaching, together with the monastic tradition it nourished, takes this absolutely seriously. The constant fidelity to the simple recitation of your word – what the East calls a *mantra* – leads us to transcend the ego and all the ego's self-consciousness and distractedness. Threatened in its very existence the ego attempts to re-assert itself – the classic and humane description of how it does so and how to persevere in the naked awareness of God is contained in the fourteenth century work *The Book of Privy Counselling* by the author of *The Cloud of Unknowing* where the same tradition is recommunicated and regenerated. What the author similarly witnesses to is the summons to complete simplicity, complete harmony of heart, mind and spirit which leads to the complete integration of the whole person. Cassian, however, like those who recommunicated the tradition after him, did not pretend that this path of simplicity was not also a very real and demanding ascesis. Indeed, he himself tells us that on first hearing the doctrine he latched onto it as a short-cut to perfection, 'short and easy'[35] as he says, but that in beginning to follow it he found it far more demanding than all his previous discursive wanderings. He discovered out of his own experience that this way was a way of total discipline that requires total attention, wholehearted other-centredness. But because of this he knew that it was the following of Christ to which he was called; the other-centredness of Jesus whose centre of consciousness was not himself but his Father.

The monastic tradition has renewed this teaching in every

34. Mt. 6:7–8.
35. *Conf.* X:14.

generation through the experience of the deep joy and peace of the pilgrimage. And it can communicate its own experience with confidence and authority because it *knows*. Listen to Cassian once more:

> For what can be more sublime and perfect than for the recollection of God to be embraced in so brief a meditation and for it, dwelling on a single verse, to escape from all the limitations of things visible and to compromise in one short word the thoughts of all our prayers.[36]

Cassian more than once stresses the point that the simplicity of this teaching makes it one of universal relevance available to all people – whether they can even read or not. Purity of heart lies close at hand for all, he says, if you can say your word with faithful and loving perseverance. Then, not only your mind but your whole person, wonderfully integrated, will achieve the one-centredness that allows the Spirit to lead us into the mystery prepared for us.

The loss and recovery of a tradition is never without its ironies. The verse Cassian recommended was the Psalmist's *Deus in adjutorium meum intende* which St Benedict, Cassian's most famous disciple, honoured by placing it as the opening versicle of the Divine Office, a place it has occupied ever since in the West. But to show you that this really is a teaching for all Christians and not just for monks I would like to show you how Simone Weil discovered the tradition through her own experience in trying to follow the pilgrimage of her spirit as faithfully as she could. The beauty of her description of this discovery is its utter simplicity and, as you will see at the end of it, her profound humility. She had not self-consciously 'studied' a tradition, indeed she probably did not know it was the tradition she had found. She simply followed her pilgrimage:

> Until last September I had never once prayed in all my life, at least not in the literal sense of the word – I had never said any words to God, either out loud or mentally. I had never

36. *Conf.* X:12.

pronounced a liturgical prayer. I had occasionally recited the
Salve Regina, but only as a beautiful poem.

Last Summer, doing Greek with T . . . , I went through
the 'Our Father' word for word in Greek. We promised each
other to learn it by heart. I do not think he ever did so, but
some weeks later, as I was turning over the pages of the
Gospel, I said to myself that since I had promised to do this
thing and it was good, I ought to do it. I did it. The infinite
sweetness of this Greek text so took hold of me that for
several days I could not stop myself from saying it over all
the time. A week afterwards I began the vine harvest. I
recited the 'Our Father' in Greek every day before work,
and I repeated it very often in the vineyard.

Since that time I have made a practice of saying it through
once each morning with absolute attention. If during the
recitation my attention wanders or goes to sleep in the minut-
est degree, I begin again until I have once succeeded in going
through it with absolutely pure attention. Sometimes it comes
about that I say it again out of sheer pleasure, but I only do
so if I really feel the impulse.

The effect of this practice is extraordinary and surprises
me every time, for, although I experience it each day, it
exceeds my expectation at each repetition.

At times the very first words tear my thoughts from my
body and transport it to a place outside space where there is
neither perspective nor point of view. The infinity of the
ordinary expanses of perception is replaced by an infinity to
the second or sometimes the third degree. At the same time,
filling every part of this infinity, there is silence, a silence
which is not an absence of sound but which is the object of a
positive sensation, more positive than that of sound. Noises,
if there are any, only reach me after crossing this silence.

Sometimes, also during this recitation or at other
moments, Christ is present with me in person, but his presence is infinitely more real, more moving, more clear than
on that first occasion when he took possession of me.

I should never have been able to take it upon myself to
tell you all this had it not been for the fact that I am going
away. And as I am going more or less with the idea of

probable death, I do not believe that I have the right to keep it to myself. For after all, the whole of this matter is not a question concerning me myself. It concerns God. I am really nothing in it at all.[37]

If a tradition ebbs and flows in history it is often because those who have set out on the pilgrimage lose heart and in trying to find a way of lessening the demands it makes on them compromise themselves. The great religious and mythical metaphor for this is falling asleep – and it is not only experienced metaphorically of course. Like the disciples on Mount Tabor and in the Garden of Gethsemani the most usual way to evade a reality that is too great for us is just to fall asleep:

> And when he rose from prayer he came to the disciples and found them sleeping for sorrow and he said to them, 'Why do you sleep? Rise and pray that you may not enter into temptation.'[38]

This episode from the Gospels reveals Jesus as the great master of prayer. His call to his disciples and to us is a call to full wakefulness. Falling asleep is the perennial temptation for the man or woman of prayer. Cassian spoke of the principal dangers in entering into true prayer in phrases such as the 'perilous peace'[39] and the 'fatal sleep'.[40] Once a person has entered into this nether world it is no easy task to summon them back to life and enlightenment. Jesus returned to his disciples in the garden and three times found them sleeping.

It is because meditation is this path of persevering wakefulness that it is quite literally the prayer of faith. And if there is one concept we should clearly focus with clear heads before we set out on the pilgrimage it is what 'faith' really means. You will remember that over the past few weeks I have often talked to you about the fundamental importance of our per-

37. Simone Weil, *Waiting on God* (London, Collins Fontana, 1973), pp. 37–9.
38. Lk. 22:45–6.
39. *Conf.* 4:7.
40. *Conf.* 10:8.

sonal response to the summons of Jesus. I have said to you that, real and powerful as is the presence of Jesus in our hearts and wonderful as is the transformation it can effect, it does not impose itself on us by force – because it is Love. It will not break through the door of our heart. We must open our heart to it. The wonderful beauty of prayer is that the opening of our heart is as natural as the opening of a flower. Just as to let a flower open and bloom it is only necessary to let it be, so if we simply *are*, if we become and remain still and silent, our heart cannot but be open: the Spirit cannot but pour through into our whole being. It is this we have been created for. It is what the Spirit has been given to us to bring about.

This, then, is the real meaning of faith: openness, perseverance in wakefulness, and commitment to the pilgrimage. The word *pistis* is common in the Gospel sayings of Jesus but nowhere in his discourses does the word just mean *belief* or *conviction*. It carries instead the meaning of *trust, faithfulness, personal loyalty*. To follow Jesus was not just to have an intellectual understanding about him but to experience his personal revelation and the dimension of spirit his person opened up for human beings and to experience this to the point of union with him and, ultimately, the Father:

> He who believes (has *pistis*) in me, believes not in me but in him who sent me.[41]

The openness and steadiness of faith in Jesus transcends every human limitation separating us from the Father's love, the source and goal of our being. No one approaches the Father except through Jesus. He is the Way. But we do not enter the Way, pursue the pilgrimage, except through faith. For St Paul faith, or our open-hearted turning towards the Lord, was the fundamental quality of the Christian experience, without which the gospel cannot save. It is, indeed, as fundamental as our very creation because, although we can say now that we *exist*, we cannot say that we are in full *being* until we have entered into fully conscious relationship, until we have turned freely toward God and thereby reciprocated love, completed the cycle

41. Jn. 13:44.

of love. In the spiritual dimension we become the person we are called to be in Christ only by that gift of ourselves, that other-centredness that is the dynamic of faith. There is nothing Pelagian about St Paul's revelation of this dynamic. We have to make the free act or choice of faith for ourself but the power to do it is in God's initiative – we can say that we have a free existence and yet believe that our being originates in and depends on God. It is this subtle mystery that St Paul evokes in his letter to the Thessalonians:

> . . . God chose you from the beginning to be saved through sanctification by the Spirit and faith in the truth.[42]

He immediately goes on to add this injunction:

> So then, brethren, stand firm and hold to the traditions you were taught by us.[43]

The mystery of faith then encompasses the central paradox of our life: that we are creatures 'chosen from the beginning' and yet that we are free to make the personal response of love and trust that will allow us to be sanctified by the spirit of our creator and indeed to become 'holy as he is holy'. Once we begin to see faith in this light the revelation of Paul's gospel appears more authoritatively rooted than ever in the reality of the human person. And his message becomes clearer: faith is the sole medium by which the Spirit is liberated in a person. Because it is faith, or other-centredness, that makes us a person. For St Paul, Christ redeemed us from the self-centred curse of the law of self-righteousness so 'that we might receive the promised Spirit through faith'.[44] By faith we open our heart to the Spirit who dwells there as the presence of the Lord in his glorious prayer to the Father: his return to the heart of the Father in the love of the Spirit. But faith is also the means by which we keep our heart open and 'stand firm and steadfast'.[45] Because of our faith, our perseverance in openness, the 'Lord

---

42. 2 Thess. 2:13.
43. Ibid. v15.
44. Gal. 3:14.
45. 1 Cor. 16:13.

who is Spirit'[46] continues to dwell in our heart 'in faith working through love'.[47]

In the monastic tradition the monk is taught that 'nothing is more important than peace of mind and unbroken purity of heart'.[48] It is this purity of heart which is truly the strength of the inner self. Purity of heart is simply faith-filled openness to the Lord Jesus – the foundation of our faith. Our pilgrimage of prayer is the pilgrimage of our life because the meaning of our life consists in the expansion of our openness to love. And so prayer is a dynamic state in which we are ever more deeply rooted by our faith. It is a movement into ever more vital realms of silence and peace, into the centre of our own being, into the heart of God. To say that our faith is ever-deepening[49] does not then imply that our beliefs are becoming more fixed and dogmatic. It means what St Paul meant when he defined the gospel as the 'saving power of God for anyone who has faith'[50] and when he declared that the way of the gospel 'starts from faith and ends in faith'.[51] It means that our openness to the indwelling Spirit who pours out the life of God in our heart is an ever-expanding receptivity: as it has to be if we are to realize ourselves fully as possessing an infinite lovability and an infinite capacity for love.

The pilgrimage of prayer is the path of faith. The recitation of your word is your pure act of faith. Once entered upon, it will progressively draw more and more of your being into itself. It will seem as if it is integrating you simply in order to possess and fill you more perfectly. And out of this essential Christian experience will flow the abundance of joy and hope proclaimed by the gospel, a rootedness in ourselves and in the reality of the redemptive power of love in human life – in short, the fullness of life that Jesus came to bring us. It does not demand merely our emotional or merely our intellectual faculties but our whole person offered as a living sacrifice in the praise of

46. Gal. 5:6.
47. Gal. 5:6.
48. *Conf.* XIX:14.
49. 2 Cor. 10:15.
50. Rom. 1:16.
51. Rom. 1:17.

mind and heart.[52] Through the mystery of this wholeness a complete revolution is effected within us:

> When anyone is united to Christ there is a new world; the old order has gone and a new order has already begun.[53]

In every age the gospel has summoned men and women to a personal verification of this claim. And ours is not the first generation to be aware of the deep discontent and uneasiness that a merely theoretical or second-hand experience can create. In fact, the monastic tradition from which I have been speaking to you originated in this discontent as a revolt against it and as a positive affirmation of the possibility of authentic knowledge and of the Christian's duty to show this possibility realized. Cassian wrote that:

> Perfection is granted to each man not because of someone else's faith but because of his own earnestness. For this is practical knowledge.[54]
>
> (a knowledge gained) by those who, led not by chattering words but by experience, measure the magnitude of grace . . . [55]

Most of what we can say about this experience is inadequate. There are simply not the words to describe reality unlimited by the boundaries of thought and imagination: to try to do so is like trying to disprove the existence of language in language! The pilgrimage of meditation is a real one but the degree of its reality is proportional to the intensity of its silence. And so it is ultimately summed up 'not in many words' but in the faithful saying of our 'one little word'.[56] Just as the mystery of God's revelation to mankind is summed up in the incarnate Word of God.

The Areopagite said that the 'movement of the soul is cyclical' yet 'possessing a kind of fixed revolution',[57] like the still

52. Rom. 12:1.
53. 2 Cor. 5:17.
54. *Conf.* XV:2.
55. *Conf.* 13:18.
56. *Cloud of Unknowing*, tr. C. Wolters, (Harmondsworth, Penguin Books, 1967), ch. 39.
57. *Divine Names*, tr. Rolt (London, SPCK, 1977), ch. 4:9.

dynamism of the Trinity. It is, indeed, hardly possible to talk of linear stages of prayer, of 'progressive stages', of *progress*. Every circle expresses the paradox that every beginning is an end and every end a beginning. What we can say of the pilgrimage has always to be subordinated to the actual practice – the practice of the word which is at the same time our guide, the sacrament of our faith and the lens that unifies our being and focuses it upon the reality within us, the lens, too, by which the light of Christ is focused in us.

When we begin to say the word we do so in the face of what seems like an insuperable stream of distraction and meaninglessness that makes us feel at one and the same time angry and silly. Abbot John Chapman of Downside warned in one of his Spiritual Letters that this sort of prayer might be called ' . . . an act of ignorance, or a sensation of idiocy'. Later he goes on, 'It makes contemplatives into idiots for the moment upon occasions.'[58] At this stage we are simply concerned with continuing to say the word. You could compare this stage to what the New Testament calls 'calling on the name' (*epi to onomati*) or to a lamp being kept shining in the dark. This is our *terminus a quo*, our point of departure in faith. In time the word becomes more familiar and it seems rather as if we are sounding it. You could compare this to the expression in the New Testament of *eis to onoma*, which denotes a movement towards the name. In the Eastern Church it is likened to the soft radiance of moonlight.[59] This is our *terminus ad quem*, our pilgrimage towards the light by faith. And then the word roots itself in our consciousness, in our heart and it is as if we are hearing it. We are now becoming truly other-centred, listening not to ourselves nor to our distractions but to the Word. We are then what the New Testament calls 'in the name' (*en to onomati*) and this is the point where the prayer of the Spirit is allowed by our faith to transcend the barriers of our divided consciousness and egotistic self-reflection. Here true prayer begins: the

58. *The Spiritual Letters of Dom John Chapman* (2nd ed., London, Sheed and Ward, 1946), no. XVII, Michaelmas 1920; cf. also *Contemplative Prayer: A few simple rules*, Appendix 1.

59. cf. *La prière de Jesus par un moine de l'église d'orient* (3rd ed., Chevetogne).

end of the journey is really the beginning and we enter with the simplicity of a child into the stream of love that has always flowed and will always flow within us. We have listened to the word in faith.

> You will do well to pay attention to this as to a lamp shining in a dark place until the day dawns and the morning star rises in your hearts.[60]

At any of these cycles of the pilgrimage we can be tempted to stop and indulge in a little self-indulgent, self-reflective reverie. Especially for our self-analytical generation, we can be tempted to cling to our self-consciousness so that we can experience the experience. But our call is to the experience itself. We can be tempted to ask how far we have got or how fast we are getting there. And this is the great danger of talking about prayer at all. But if these are the hazards and the dangers on your pilgrimage there is one response to them all: fidelity to your word.

We meditate in order to become wholly silent, wholly conscious. We begin in faith, we persevere in faith. But there is no end because love has no end and our faith, our prayer itself, is our openness to love.

I hope these talks have helped you to a deeper understanding of the priority of the experience of prayer in any human life that can be called fully human or fully alive. I hope they have communicated to you the urgent need that the Church has today for men and women of prayer who can communicate the word and power of the gospel through the reality of the love of God in the human heart. But above all, I hope that they may lead you, in the pattern of your own life that only God knows, to enter more richly into the experience of the mystery of Jesus.

The summary of the monastic tradition of prayer that I have tried to put before you is, of course, little more than a sketch of a rich all-pervasive experience. But in order to make it a living tradition it is not necessary to study it so much as to practise it, to live its vision in our own lives. This is the chal-

---

60. 2 Pet. 1:19.

113

lenge to the Church and particularly to monasticism today: not to write monographs on prayer but to produce people committed to a life of prayer in the fullness of the tradition. The wonderful thing about the monastic life when it is really lived like this is that it cannot help but communicate its experience to all around it and to lead all who come into contact with it to participate in this mystery.

Those of you who have come into contact with our Benedictine Community here in Montreal will, I hope, have seen that there is nothing esoteric or exclusive about this tradition. The participation of the Lay Community and the weekly meditation groups in the prayer-life of the monastic tradition is a focal point of the Christian tradition, of the Christian experience of prayer, lived with a particular kind of commitment. But because the essence and fruit of this tradition is the love of God its response and relation to all reality is expansive.

I have talked a lot and sometimes quite elaborately. But let me end by reminding you that nothing can be said about prayer that can at the same time describe its utter fullness and its utter simplicity. I suggest you now forget most of what I have said except the two words 'simplicity' and 'faith' – and both of these are summed up in the practice of the one word that will allow you to be led by the Spirit. I have not suggested to you that the simplicity is easy to reach or the faith easy to maintain. But let me remind you again that this condition of wholehearted openness to love is the condition to which you and I and every human being is called. It demands everything. But in the end all you will lose are your limitations. So may we 'attain to fullness of being, the fullness of God himself'.[61]

61. Eph. 3:19.

The Monastic Adventure

Preface

I remember seeing the response of a group of monks to whom John Main was talking about the renewal of monasticism in the face of the challenge presented by a post-religious society. He spoke with a calm passion and a deep sense of urgency. Most of his listeners looked uncomfortable, even embarrassed. As a monk John Main had the disturbing prophetic quality of upsetting our complacency about the future by his penetrating vision of the present.

Monasticism, for him, was an adventure of the Spirit, not one monks chose themselves but one into which the Spirit led them. It was an ever-fresh and ever-expanding way of responding to the gospel at the deepest personal level. Because this was how he experienced his monastic vocation John Main lived it with an apparently unlimited energy. To live the monastic life with him, as so many of his brethren discovered from his earliest days as a novice, was often to be swept up with an energy of joy and vitality that revealed the real nature of monastic peace and stability.

He saw monasticism as being renewed by a rediscovery of its contemplative tradition and also by responding to the spiritual crisis of our society out of the lived practice of this tradition. He knew that a new kind of monastery and monk were being called into being. But rooted in the tradition and its contemporary application, he also knew that the new monk would perhaps be more recognizable to the founders of the tradition than might at first appear. The discoveries and opportunities of monasticism we discovered in the first years in Montreal have revealed themselves as profoundly inserted in the monastic continuum.

As the monk pursues his (or her) own vocation he serves his

brethren everywhere. He sees all humanity as his family. He contributes a vital, immeasurable dividend to the commonwealth of society. It is always surprising to realize that he does so because of the discovery of love in his own being, in his communion with the brethren in the monastery, in his availability to the world. It was because this love was so real a force and presence in his life that John Main pointed beyond all images of monasticism, all monk-acting. He saw and pointed into the pure experience of monasticism and so revealed its universal quality. He knew this power of love to be at the same time liberating for the individual, leading to fullness of life in Christ, and profoundly civilizing for society, contributing to the peace and trust so desperately needed in our human family today.

Laurence Freeman osb

The Witness to the World of Monastic Prayer

Fifteen hundred years after the death of St Benedict, monasticism today has as great an opportunity as it has ever had to witness to the absolute value of a life centred in Christ.

The life of the monk witnesses, *points to*, a new creation that is already among us and around us, a spiritual reality that we can see only with the vision that comes from a pure heart. His life witnesses to the great fact of this creation, namely that God and only God is to be worshipped because he alone is all goodness and his goodness does not pass away like the world but endures for all eternity. Loving God, worshipping God, is the call to us to be open to our own eternal potential in God, in the new creation whose centre is Christ. The monk is one who humbly searches for the way to realize this potentiality.

In the celebration of all anniversaries the temptation is to look back to the glories of the past. And certainly every Benedictine monk is someone with a sense of tradition. But, as Kierkegaard said unforgettably, only that past which can be made a present reality is worth remembering. A monk is a man who can carry the past with him, *collect* it on his pilgrimage and transform it into the radiant present of the new creation. The monk is therefore a man who must make his tradition more relevant to the present than mere novelty.

In this talk I want to put before you what seems to me to lie at the centre of the contemporary challenge to monks. Our call is to be people of prayer. Our life of prayer is our fundamental apostolate. It seems to me to be the supreme importance of monastic prayer that it is a tangible sign to the world of the reality of God's presence in our midst. And further, it seems to me that because of this the monk by his wholehearted search for God has enormous importance for contemporary men and women. His message arises from his life itself. It is a message of profound significance because it arises from the depth of his own personal commitment. His message to his brothers and sisters is this: 'Lift up your hearts. Open your eyes to what is real, to the new creation. Seek the purity of heart that opens your eyes. Understand and know in your own heart that you were created for infinite expansion of spirit.' His message is that these are not idealistic cries but entirely realistic possibilities for you, for each of us, if we are open to the experience of Jesus. There is urgency and immediateness in this message: every morning St Benedict had his monks recite the words of the psalm, 'Oh, that *today* you would hear his voice.'

But one of our problems is the problem of language. It is not enough to hear the challenge expressed as someone else's experience. Each one of us has to come to grips with these realities as men and women of our own time. One of the key words that can help to bring these realities into our own present experience is a key Christian word and, therefore, a key monastic word – 'conversion'. The Christian is one who is converted to Christ, turned to Christ at the centre of his or her being. The monk is one who seeks to live this conversion as the main thrust of his life.

Unless we understand what is really meant by this ancient word 'conversion' I think we are going to fail to understand the challenge facing monasticism and, indeed, the Church today. We have heard the word so often that perhaps for many of us it has lost its power to convey its full meaning, its power, namely, to turn us around – to turn us to Christ.

I believe that all of us, monks and lay people, will better understand the New Testament and St Benedict if we can begin to see conversion to Christ in terms of transcendence in Christ. Transcendence has to be understood as an expansion of your being, a pushing back of the frontiers of your limitations. It is a dynamic motion beyond ourselves in which we leave limitation behind and enter into a creative development of our whole being – a deepening of the integral harmony of heart and mind. In this movement of transcendence we begin to find our own true significance as beings created for an eternal destiny in union with God. We no longer understand ourselves or our lives in terms of our limitations but rather in terms of our potentiality for expansion, indeed for infinite expansion. This is the invitation we each have as Christians, the invitation namely to leave self behind and to enter into this expansion and find *fullness of being* as St Paul expresses it. As Christians we have the insight that this fullness of being results from our awareness of God in Jesus. And that means our human consciousness open to the human consciousness of Jesus dwelling in our hearts. This is our way to the Father.

This is, too, the thrust of the words of St Paul:

> Be strong to grasp with all God's people what is the breadth and length and height and depth of the love of Christ and to know it, though it is beyond knowledge. So may you attain to fullness of being, the fullness of God himself. (Eph. 3:14)

At the beginning of our look at monastic prayer as witness, let us all be absolutely clear on this – every one of us, all monks and all Christians, are called to this fullness of being, the fullness of God himself. And, furthermore, we are each called to it by the same process of transcendence – transcending our own limited life through our experiencing the life, the love, of Jesus.

But again we must face the question of meaning. What does it mean for us as men and women of the twentieth century to say that our call is to experience the love of Christ? What does it mean to say that the call to transcendence for each of us is the call to be fully ourselves – to be wholly *real*? One thing is clear, that the answers to these questions are not going to be adequately made in any of the terms of psychology, sociology or even theology. St Paul himself tells us that the experience they refer to is beyond our normal terms of reference, beyond the limits of our usual analytical approach to experience. He tells us this when he tells us that we must know the love of Christ '*though it is beyond knowledge*'. And in these words he indicates that the experience is one of transcendence. Let us remember again that transcendence involves not the remote or unreal but the fully real, the fullness of being. St Paul says it is 'beyond knowledge'. In other words, as our tradition tells us, we can only know God with his own self-knowledge. We must leave our knowledge behind and enter into his knowledge.

The monastery exists precisely to provide the incarnate and participatory context in which the love of Christ can be known. In the monastery this expansion of spirit, this transcendence or passing over away from self to the other, can be known by experiencing it, by sharing in it. It can be shared precisely because it is *real*, not just an ideal, and because its reality is incarnated in a fully human and loving community.

In traditional monastic language the *reality* of a monastery depends upon its conversion – its *'conversatio'* which for Benedict meant a lifelong turning, an ongoing conversion. In our own day this still applies and indeed constitutes much of the challenge monasticism faces. We can only understand what a monastery is if we know it as a community which has found its common ground and fraternal inspiration in a shared knowledge of conversion. The monks have come to know that their community is constituted by their commitment to conversion. And they know that conversion is turning from themselves to their brethren in community; and to Christ in prayer; and to God in Christ. This is the Benedictine tradition. When it is fully alive in the present it has the power to convert the hearts of all who come under its influence.

For a truly contemporary expression of this monastic dynamic we have to return to the word 'transcendence'. We have to understand a monastery as a human community striving for transcendence – 'seeking God' as Benedict put it. They strive for a continual expansion of spirit and ever growing generosity. They seek, as a community, for ongoing growth and development in their understanding of Christ's presence in their midst as the supreme, the foundational reality. They seek and strive for these things as their first priority. And the place they seek and strive in is the monastery. Monks are not committed to abstract ideas or ideals in the first place but to the human reality that constitutes their community. In that community they find the first spark of love that their life of prayer and fraternity fans into the fire of God's reality. As St John tells us, no one has ever seen God – but we can all experience God whenever and wherever we encounter love.

Monks, like all of us, can be held captive by certain illusions. We are all given to striving for worthless goals and we are all, to a greater or lesser extent, given over to projecting the right sort of image of ourselves to the world. These are universal human characteristics, not just secular ones. It is against these that the movement of transcendence you find in a monastery is directed. The process of transcendence is a passing beyond all these illusions, all these images. It is the supreme movement from image to reality. It is the conversion, in the heart of a person, of idea into reality. The reality is God and only in his light can each of us become wholly real. Without his light we would not even know we are called to realize our potential, to become real. Because we do know it through his gift of light, our movement of transcendence, of conversion, is not centred in ourselves but in him. Because he is our centre, the power of transcendence comes from him and not from our own spiritual ambition. The love we experience in our monastic life is not our love for God but his love for us.

The experience of prayer is the experience of the liberating consequences of transcendence. It is, as I have said, transcendence realized. What happens in prayer is that the love of Christ is set free in our hearts. All the illusions and images that restrict or distort it are transcended. It is a work of finding and realizing our own human freedom, our freedom from desire, from sin, from illusion. Only if we are free and so restored to our divine likeness can we know the love of Christ. Our freedom is the condition of our being real, being in harmonious contact with the ground of our being, our source and origin. The ground of our being is reached only by the movement of other-centredness, of transcendence. Following that movement, led by the Spirit, we enter the experience of becoming wholly real within God's own free-flowing and all-embracing reality.

These are high claims, not just for a monastery but for human nature. Discussion of them has only a limited value unless there has been some degree of the experience that they *are* totally justified claims. A society that is losing this experience is a society that, losing its faith, is also losing its own centre, its own reality. 'Things fall apart, the centre cannot hold, mere anarchy is loosed upon the world, and everywhere the ceremony of innocence is drowned.' (W.B. Yeats, *The Second Coming*.)

The essentially civilizing power of monasticism in the past was not the quiet scribes copying the manuscripts of a threatened culture nor was it the patronage of the arts by the great monasteries. The essential contribution of monks to their civilization is always that they form a community of love in which the centre not only holds but continually expands. The vitality of its centredness passes over into every aspect of its life and makes of its life what Yeats' phrase could be used to describe the truly Christian civilization – 'the ceremony of innocence'.

We must, therefore, understand the monastery as a Christian community of prayer, centred in Christ. Such a community can never find its ultimate meaning within its own limitations. The essential meaning of the monastery is always found beyond itself. Every life and every monastery that is truly Christian must always find its ultimate meaning by finding its centre in the Lord of the new creation. For it is the Lord who eternally holds the initiative by having called the community into being and by calling it to serve him. A Christian community is one living its conversion – turned beyond itself – always and ever more open to the transcendent Lord who summons it into the fullness of being, the fullness of God himself.

We are now ready to say what the great witness of monastic life is to the world. We know it is not just a spectacle that the world can observe for relaxation or consolation. The monastic witness is something that attracts attention but also *participation*. It is more of a ceremony than a spectacle – but a ceremony in which people begin to understand a great truth about themselves that they had not before actually believed to be real. A monastery can reveal to the world what it did not know and it can verify what the world only tentatively believes. It can do this out of the power of its movement of transcendence. Its rootedness in Christ is its confidence and its authority. It is because its transcendent character is so dynamic a reality that it creates a vortex of love that draws men and women into the mystery of God. The monastery does this by the power of the Risen Lord made present by its own living faith.

In traditional monastic wisdom the purpose of such a Christian community of prayer is twofold. In the first place its purpose is the realization of its union with the Lord: the knowledge that Christ's love flows freely at its centre, and the experience of the liberty and joy that comes from that knowledge. In the second place, its purpose is to create the context within which this realization may be pursued as its very first responsibility – and pursued by the most practical means possible.

This is the wisdom expressed in traditional language: 'The end of our profession indeed, as I have said, is the Kingdom of God or the Kingdom of Heaven: but the immediate aim or goal is purity of heart, without which no one can gain that end.' (Cassian, *Conf.* I:iv)

To understand the challenge facing the monastic tradition today we have again to find a contemporary expression of this wisdom. And so we have to understand, to begin with, that the Kingdom of God is not a place but rather an experience. Because our understanding of the nature of prayer is so often distorted by our imagination this is not always an easy insight to hold on to. But it is vital. Our childhood education about heaven as a 'place we go to after we die' and about prayer as 'telling God what we want' has enormous and enduring influence on us. But we have to awaken to the major limitations of this education, designed, as it was, for children. So often our spiritual maturity falls far behind our other levels of growth and development. And this is perhaps why Benedict called his monastery a 'school of the Lord's service' because it was a place where people would be able to learn to mature in Christ, in the depths of their being. For Benedict knew that if people were immature in spirit they would be unfulfilled at every other level too. But mature in spirit, through their experience of transcendence, they would have the power to teach, lead and inspire others in the mysteries of the Kingdom.

The Kingdom of God has to be understood today not as a place but as an experience. It is the experience of the power of God, of the power of his love. When Cassian says that the purpose of the monastic life is the Kingdom of God he is saying that, for the monk, the aim of life is that the power of God's love become the supreme reality. To be open to that love is to be open to all. The monk is simply a person who seeks to be open, as the grounding experience of his life, to God's love – the basic energy of all creation.

Cassian was an eminently practical man. He goes on to say that we cannot achieve this aim, cannot enter the experience without what he calls 'purity of heart'. The practicality of his teaching becomes clearer if we understand that purity of heart is, quite simply, the state of undivided consciousness. It is the state we are in when we are in love, wholly turned towards the one we love. It is the state, too, of being wholly at one with the work or creative act in which we are involved. In monastic terms, it is the state of pure openness to God beyond all division, beyond all desire. Purity of heart is a state transcending division and desire because there is no room in us for these *unreal* things. We are filled to fullness with the reality of God. It is the aim and purpose of our monastic prayer to bring us to such purity of heart, such a state of undistracted concentration – to the pure awareness of God in Jesus. And because prayer has to be understood in this context our approach to prayer has to be practical and realistic.

If this is the reality of a monk's life, then it is his unique and invaluable witness to the world. His life of prayer encourages all to enter this fullness of being because his witness is not witness to a beautiful theory or to theological poetry. He witnesses to a present reality, and he does so because he is committed to the reality of the transcendent Presence that summons him to an infinite expansion of spirit. His life is a journey of conversion that leads him out of the realm of religious ideas and ideals into the reality that St Paul describes as 'God with us'. The important question that every person and every generation has to ask in the face of the claim of the gospel is, 'Is this journey really possible for us who are ordinary, very ordinary, men and women?'

The monk answers this question with his life. It is in answering it that it seems to me that monasticism – or should I say monks – have their vital contribution to make to our world. When men and women in the world ask if this inner journey is possible, monks must be able to reply in the words of Jesus, 'Come and see.' We invite you to come to our monastery and share our prayer – our experience of the Kingdom. Come and share this journey into the knowledge that is Love.

This is the essential *hospitality* of the monk and his community, his radical openness and benevolence to all. He does not serve the world by condemning it or by setting up a false opposition between world and cloister. He serves rather by his prophetic humility, by inviting the world unilaterally to join him in his experience of God in Jesus. In this sense the monk's experience is a self-communicating experience. He is a man of the gospel not in the first place by teaching or preaching but rather by *being* – by being the man he is called to be. And that is a man rooted in God and living directly out of the power of his rootedness, his centredness.

The simplicity of a monk as a person, like the simplicity of his community's lifestyle, is designed to allow the essential quality of his being to communicate itself as directly as possible. The monk and the monastery seek a style and structure that will offer as little distortion as possible to the free passage of the light that burns at the centre of the monastic spirit. For this reason he simplifies his life by a radical process of detachment from mundane concerns to allow his roots to sink ever deeper into the absolute concern that directs him, the mystery of God. His detachment is an essential element in the experience of conversion or transcendence that becomes more and more real as he grows in purity of heart. His detachment becomes the ground then of his spontaneity, his alertness, his capacity to respond to the reality of his situation. He has no barriers around him. As Evagrius said of monks, they are detached from all and so they are in harmony with all. To this process of detachment the monk must devote all the energy of his love. It is in this process that the transcendence which is the dynamic of his prayer is to be found. And in his prayer the monk is at his most detached for he is detached not just from the world but from his own self. And so it is in his prayer that he is in complete harmony – at one with God, with himself and with all people and in this state of oneness, of communion, of growing rootedness in love, his witness is most vital, most self-communicating.

In ancient monastic wisdom the monk was enjoined to 'fly

from the world'. The inevitable process by which all absolute spiritual teaching seems to get diluted or compromised over the centuries, eventually came to present this as a negative, self-indulgent or romantic option. But what I have said should, I hope, make it clear just how positive, other-centred and realistic it is. His flight from the world, his detachment, has one purpose: to allow him to become totally available for the basic Christian experience. His openness to God in Jesus makes his 'flight from the world' his most valuable contribution to the world. A monk living his life in faith is an incarnation of the love of Jesus.

That does not mean the monk is a superman. He is an ordinary Christian who lives his life in the centre of the Christian community. And everything about monasticism that is really part of the living tradition points to the fact that it is ordinary Christian life – but lived with an extraordinary fidelity. The relationship between the ordinary and the extraordinary in monasticism is vital to its witness: the relationship ensures that the monastery is neither limited by the world nor alienated from it. This is of course a delicate balance that only discretion in the actual situation can achieve and maintain. When it is found and held, though, the monastic life is a transforming call to ordinary Christians to awaken to the extraordinary gift that is theirs: Christ among you. In hearing this call from monks the contemporary Christian is presented with a challenge similar to that facing the monks and asking for a similar response of faith. The challenge is simply to respond to the invitation of Christ made to each of us in our own name. No one can make another person's response for him or her. No one can make the journey for you. All Christians have to respond to the call that the monk can help them hear and do so with a love that takes them beyond the mundane, the materialistic, the trivial, into the infinite depths of God.

Monastic maturity is persuasive. It encourages others who encounter it to accept the same call as the central priority of their life. But before it can do that it has to be truly central to the monk's life. St Benedict asks of whoever comes to be a monk that, as the first condition, he really seeks God. The test of it in the novice, we are told, is perseverance and steadiness in prayer. This is not just a pre-condition of entering the monastery, not just a first hurdle to the 'status' of being a monk. It is the foundation stone of the whole of his monastic life – of monasticism. It is this search for God that is the great witness of monastic prayer. By making the search in all seriousness, joy and humility our function in the Church and the world alike is to say to all men and women of goodwill: the fullness of life you read about in the New Testament concerns you, is vital to you and is a present possibility for you.

St Benedict also spoke of progress in monastic life as a progress in faith. Faith, again, is a word that has lost its edge for most of us. For the writers of the New Testament 'faith' means something more than belief. It is personal commitment, perseverance, self-giving. It is steadiness through the ups and downs of life and of our psychological responses to life. This is the sense St Benedict has of the word when he says the monk is a person of faith. He is someone who is faithful to the journey he has begun to follow. He is committed to that openness which is a progression from the limitations of self into the limitless life of God.

In the Prologue to the Rule Benedict tells us that this progress creates an expansion of heart that opens up the possibility of still more progress and is accompanied by a delight of love that is beyond description. St Gregory of Nyssa had the same vision of the Christian life as an entry into the infinite expansion of God, God's endless creativity. What Benedict and Gregory were trying to say – only *trying*, because of course it cannot be said, it can only be known – is of great significance to the challenge facing monasticism today. To meet the challenge, to deepen their faith in their vocation, monks have to understand more clearly than ever that this infinite expansion is rooted in the concrete, finite situation of their life. That is to say, it is really *possible*. But to realize the possibility they have to face the facts of their present situation head-on, unflinchingly. And they have to remain facing them with the stability of heart that Benedict gives as an essential characteristic of the monastic response. They have to be still. In the stillness they will find the moment of transcendence in which their faith will take them beyond ideas into reality, beyond images into knowledge.

St Gregory said that prayer is a journey unlike all other jour-
neys. If we want to travel from Cleveland to Montreal we have
to move from A to B. But if we make the journey of prayer
we do so by becoming still. The progress is in the stillness.
Accepting the stillness of the *now* leads us into the *eternal*. I
think this is what Simone Weil meant, too, when she said that
the only way we can transcend our limitations is by accepting
them. All these are different ways of saying that faith is the
matrix of the monastic life. The monk's perseverance in prayer
regardless of his circumstances of life or his feelings, his commitment to stability and stillness, his acceptance of the concrete
reality of his situation – all these are what we call his faith.
And his witness is a witness of faith, too, because what he
communicates depends upon its own self-communicating power
and is not primarily dependent on what he teaches or preaches.
This makes it clear how closely faith is tied in with that other
great monastic quality – silence. The test and sign of faith is
silence. A silence that is neither sullenness or timidity. A
silence that speaks for itself.

The witness of a monastery, then, is a witness of faith. It is
not as perhaps we imagine it, a witness to mere endurance,
mere doggedness. The faith is joy-filled and love-filled. But it
is not triumphalist. The faith is also filled with wonder at the
infinite expansion that is taking place in the monk's heart. The
moderation, the sanity of a monastery that nurtures this faith
is a delicate and vital quality. It is a rejection of all fanaticism
as well as a balanced acceptance of extremism. Monks *are*
extremists. They have made an absolute response to an absolute call. They are fools for Christ's sake. But they are not
fanatics. Their rules of life are all subservient to the great
principle of charity and discretion – a discretion that leads to
maturity rather than a legalism that leads to infantilism – this
is their 'rule', their yardstick.

A monastery truly in touch with its own tradition as a contemporary reality will be one that knows that the prayer of the
monk is the well-spring of his inspiration – and his inspiration
is the witness that can inspire others. The prayer of the monk
is not an abstract witness. It is a *daily* manifestation of faith
rooted in love.

The challenge to monks of our own time is to enter into a way of prayer that arises from our own specifically monastic tradition and yet is also one entirely credible for twentieth century society. This is the balance between tradition and modernity that can only be found by making the tradition entirely present in personal experience. If we point to the tradition as something relevant and important, we can hardly expect to be taken seriously if we speak merely of history. In bringing the power of our tradition before our contemporaries as something that can help us in our predicament we have to be pointing to something fully relevant here and now, but we can do this only when we speak from living tradition – from present experience.

The monastic life is designed to make this possible. The elements of monastic living as described in the Rule are three-fold: Oratio, prayer; Lectio, reading; Labor, work. The monastic life, to be sane and healthy, requires that each of these elements is present and that the three together are kept in balance so that one does not displace another. Once they are in balance they have to be kept in a balance that does not become a deadening routine. And this can only be avoided, legalism can only be avoided, if they are bound together by a vital fraternal love.

In the monastery it should be plain for all to see that the conversion of the monk is a passing over from the monk's limited experience into the unlimited experience, the wholly awakened consciousness of Jesus. What I would like to do now, very briefly, is to suggest how each of these three elements of the monastic life leads to this condition of transcendence. Once we can see that clearly, the essential witness of monastic prayer stands out in sharp perspective.

St Benedict saw Lectio, reading, as an integral part of our Christian living. Why? Not because it made us better conversationalists or helped us pass exams. The purpose of Lectio in the monastery is not the acquisition of knowledge. And it is important to emphasize this because we have been trained to regard all education as the amassing of knowledge as a form of power.

His Lectio is another exercise in self-transcendence. The monk is not trying to possess what he studies but uses his study to help him respond to the presence of God in his Word. All of us, of course, are called to this knowledge of God in his revealed Word and for the same reason – so that we may discover his living Word in our hearts. A loving reading and reflection upon the Word of Scripture is, in Benedict's vision, essential in forming the monk as a man of prayer.

To pray is to be open to the otherness of God. To love is to turn beyond self towards another. What summons us to this turning, this conversion or self-transcendence, is the Word of God. The text of Scripture before us leads us into the otherness of God and the monk faithful to his reading of Scripture has more capacity to witness to the reality of that otherness found in the living person of Jesus – the Person who lives in our hearts, the *inner man* of each of us. Lectio, like every other aspect of the monastic life, is there to prepare us for the encounter with this Person, for contact with his otherness. And more than contact, for it prepares us for the movement of transcendence right beyond ourselves and into the life of the Trinity, the communion of God, the mutual love that is God. Lectio prepares us for the mystery of God – a mystery that 'eye has not seen, nor ear heard'. We have to be clear that it does *prepare* us. The movement itself is accomplished by the redemptive love of Jesus that we encounter as our spirit opens fully to his life released in our hearts.

Our prayer *is* our openness of heart. We prepare to open our hearts by the fundamental quality of simplicity that we bring to our Lectio. The simplicity of the monk, as I have said, is his way to oneness with Jesus. And so, Lectio is the great preparation for prayer that each monk builds into his life. It is also built into the corporate community life in the form of Community Lectio and this is what we know as the Divine Office. The Office is, for the monks in assembly, their attentive, daily reading of the sacred texts of Scripture and the traditional interpretation of those texts by the Church through the ages. It is always a sacred moment in the monastic day when the monks as one person, one in Christ, listen to the Word addressed to them. It is a moment that St Benedict called monks to return to seven times a day.

It is, I think, essential that we understand the Divine Office as this *preparation* for prayer if we are to recover our monastic balance in the three elements of our life. Upon this balance depends our making-present the full richness of our tradition and so also our relevance to the world. This is in no way to play down the sacredness of the Divine Office. Quite the reverse, what it reveals is the true meaning and effective value of the Office as the great community context for preparing the heart of each monk to be open to the same reality. It prepares them for the prayer that is the unity they share. It prepares them for the encounter with the otherness of God in silence and stillness – in what St Benedict calls in the Rule, '*oratio pura*' – pure prayer. That is the prayer that is beyond thought, beyond imagination, beyond words – the prayer in which we are *simply* in the presence.

Monastic work is a similar schooling in otherness because it leads the monk to find Christ everywhere and in everyone. Hence, the spirit of love and perfection he brings to it. The work he does is the work he is given to do and what this should be is always evident when the priority is not the search for self-fulfilment but the search for God, a search that is centred in his life of prayer. The service of the monastery to the world, then, is both the fruit of its prayer and its preparation for prayer. All roads in the monastery lead to prayer, to Benedict's sense of *oratio pura*.

The phrase 'pure prayer' Benedict takes from one great source for his Rule, John Cassian. In the twentieth chapter of the Rule he summarizes what Cassian had taught about monastic prayer by saying that it consists not in much speaking but in purity of heart. This pure prayer is a going-beyond words, a going-beyond thoughts, a going-beyond all imagination. It is a transcendence of these and all other limitations and an arriving at stillness within the infinite love of God. Cassian taught Benedict that this prayer was not anything esoteric. It was the common monastic destiny and was not beyond the resources of ordinary people. Being unsophisticated or even illiterate was no barrier to entering it.

Cassian's and Benedict's confidence still inspire us to make the tradition they transmit live again in our day. And what gives *us* confidence is to realize that what they teach is precisely their insight that the resources necessary for this journey are infinite when the monk has his or her centre in Christ. The other-centredness of monastic prayer is perhaps its primary characteristic. Indeed, for St Anthony, the monk who was still so centred in himself that he knew he was praying was not really praying because he was not *wholly* absorbed in God. His remark, quoted by Cassian, emphasizes that Christian prayer cannot be a self-conscious occupation. Nor, in the monastic tradition, is it trying to make something happen. Rather, it is simply being still enough, being humble enough and being poor enough to realize what is *already* happening. Wisdom, the offspring of prayer, consists simply in understanding what IS. And the monk, by his *simplicity*, his *silence* and his *stillness* is a sign to all people of what IS around them and within them: his witness is to the God who IS.

All the dispositions of the Rule are made to dispose the heart of the monk for his experience of Being in the experience of pure prayer. The challenge facing every monk and monastery is to ensure that the balance of all these dispositions, symbolized in the three elements of the Rule, is held at the service of prayer as the first monastic priority: the basic experience of each of the monks.

The monk, by essential definition, is one who is continuously on guard against distraction and shallowness. Not in theory but in practice, he returns throughout the day and each day to the centre of reality by continually focusing his life's aim in the experience of Jesus. As Jesus is centred in the Father so the monk is centred in Jesus and shares his dynamic stability in the great stream of love flowing between Jesus and the Father. This is not just *part* of his life. It is the structure of his life and after a lifetime in the monastery it is the structure of his being.

The pure prayer of a monk is not just an activity he adds to other functions. It is the condition of his being out of which all his action springs and he places it, therefore, before all action. For our modern mind, so geared to the priority of action, this seems reckless, perhaps even irresponsible. But it is the great witness of monastic prayer. The prayer of the monk arises from his faith that the Kingdom is already established – among us and within our hearts. His daily commitment to silence, to wholeness, to the basic conversion of life by which we turn from creation to Creator in a transcendent movement of love – this releases the spiritual energy of the new creation brought into being by Christ.

Our life as monks is founded on the central Christian revelation: that Jesus is both the co-eternal Word of God and fully human. Because he is both he has been able to lift us out of our isolation and into the experience of communion with God that is both his experience and our fullness of being. This he does in the present moment – the eternal moment of transcendence – by dwelling in our heart in the fullness of his being as God and as man. In our heart, in our inmost being, his glorified human consciousness makes contact with our consciousness in redeeming love. He opens his spirit to ours and so becomes our way to the Father. The monastic life of prayer is the realization of this as *the* foundational truth: 'May you know it, though it is beyond knowledge and so may you attain to fullness of being, the fullness of God himself.'

The journey to this fullness is an expansion of our capacity to infinity. But it is a way that demands discipline, concentration and devotion. A major part of the witness of the monk's life of prayer is to make the monastery a centre and source of this discipline and selfless love. It makes a context in which people of faith really do seek God. The wonder of the monastery both for monks and the world, is that others have heard the same absolute call and have responded to it. In a world increasingly ravaged by loneliness and isolation, the monastery is a practical demonstration that this is not the inevitable lot of human beings. It shows that we are called into the joy of being and in the living witness of flesh and blood it reveals being itself as communion.

Every aspect of the monastic witness is paradoxical. It can, therefore, never be explained or justified as other, more conventional lifestyles can be. But perhaps its most paradoxical and valuable witness is to be found in the word 'monk' itself. It comes from the Greek word *monos*. The monk is one. He has become one with his own spirit and so with all people and with God. He has found the wholeness of his being in his union with Christ. A monk is above all a man called to oneness and he responds to this above all other calls. And it is his oneness that is his principal witness to the world. In the prayer of monks the words of Jesus have come alive ' . . . may they all be one, as thou Father art in me and I in them, so may they also be in us, that the world may believe that thou didst send me.' (Jn 17:20)

Benedictine Prayer

It is no exaggeration, in describing St Benedict as the perfect monk, to see him as pre-eminently a 'man for others'. In his Rule this comes through clearly in his vision of the monastic family as a fraternity of mutual love and mutual obedience or sensitivity – a truly Christian community in which each must be concerned with the other and not with himself. This is the basic orientation of St Benedict's monastery and it is this that constitutes it as a community of those who would pray.

To stress this community nature of the monastic adventure may at first seem a strange emphasis in discussing Benedictine prayer. Yet, the precise strength and wisdom of St Benedict's understanding of the way to prayer is in his firm grasp of St John's theology of fraternal love in his First Letter.

> And indeed this command comes to us from Christ himself as he who loves God must also love his brother. (1 John 4:21)

The strength of monastic community lies in this fact that we come to know ourselves in the perfecting relationships that we establish with our brothers and sisters and each one of these relationships is itself a sacrament of our fundamental relationship with Christ and his Father in the Holy Spirit. Christ's incarnation reveals to us the fullness of that relationship in his total love for his Father and his total love for us – 'even to death on the cross'. A monastic vocation is a call to explore this fundamental relationship to the full – at whatever cost to ourselves.

St Benedict's Rule is built on this awareness that we exist *in relationship*. And not just in self-interested relationship where we put our own perfection or religious routine before the concern we have for our brothers or sisters in our monastic family.

This would be that self-centred deformed relationship which Sartre described in the phrase 'hell is other people'. This we can describe as a 'deformed relationship' because instead of being a perfecting meeting with another in the context of true community it is merely an awareness of our own isolated juxta-position in the crowd.

Religious communities must therefore understand fully the difference between the *crowd* and the *true community*. In our lives we attempt to live out and explore to its depths mankind's invitation to enter into community with *the* community of love – the most holy Trinity. The crowd is first defined to my knowl-edge by Kierkegaard. He said, 'The crowd in its very concept is the untruth by reason of the fact that it renders the individual completely impenitent and irresponsible.'

Kierkegaard saw into this anonymous leviathan so clearly and he was so horrified that in his recoiling he perhaps over-emphasized the independence of the individual. Nevertheless his writings still bring hope to those submerged in the lonely crowd.

But thinkers who followed in the existentialist tradition have attempted to redress the balance and have shown us the essen-tial paradox of our independent existence in community. Nevertheless the crowd remains as a sign of contradiction. Heidegger, for example, re-expressed it as 'das man' – the *they*. He defines it even better than Kierkegaard, perhaps, in saying 'Everyone is the other and no one is himself.'

The strength of Christian community is that when everyone is *for the other* everyone becomes himself or herself. The com-munity lives out Christ's insight that the 'person who would find his life must lose it'. In other words, the real self is found in community and not in the crowd. The anxious and suffering self glorified by decadent romanticism is the fantasy of our existence that oppresses us, as long as we live in a crowd and live for its self-protecting fears.

And here we come to a fundamental difference between the crowd and community. The crowd is always enclosing and engulfing those who are drawn into it. In a crowd we experience our own personal self as limited and limiting. We are possessed by the mentality of the mob. In community, on the other hand, the experience is one of liberation. The community is always pointing the way ahead, beyond the self. It is not the final form – there are always greater, deeper community experiences ahead. St Benedict's own conviction of the hermitage beyond the monastic community is a prime example of the self-transcending nature of the true Christian community. The reason is this – the crowd always exists for its own sake. It seeks to swallow up more and more and thus become a more and more significant crowd. The community on the other hand always exists for those who form it. Its purpose is to help its members grow and, as St Benedict foresaw, if that growth proceeds sufficiently the members will grow beyond the community itself.

The call then of the monastic adventure is to live in community more deeply, more extremely. In this experience of exploring our relation with the other we come to realize that there is in essence one relationship, one community. Teilhard de Chardin once said when talking about the Eucharist, 'all communions are one communion'. And this surely is what St John meant when he said, 'He who loves lives in God and God lives in him.' The particular end of the monastic life is to become aware of this one relationship. How do we do so?

W.H. Auden once wrote that the primary task of the school teacher is to teach children, in the secular context, the technique of prayer.[1] By this he meant the capacity to concentrate wholly on something or someone other than oneself – to become wholly attentive to the inner coherence of a poem, to become absorbed in the harmonious tonality of a picture, to appreciate the logical completeness of a mathematical problem, to see the delicate structure of a leaf under a microscope. Each one of these experiences enables the student to transcend his or her own limited self, to forget his or her own ego and desires and to pass over into the experience of concentrating on the other.

St Benedict calls the monastery a school and it is a school wherein we too have to learn this primary lesson – to concentrate upon the other, to leave behind our own false ego and all our desire. St Benedict's way is quite simple. In order to teach us to love the God whom we cannot see he asks us to

1. *A Certain World, A Commonplace Book* (1970).

begin by loving our neighbour whom we can see. In other words his Johannine view is that if we cannot concentrate upon our neighbour we will not be able to concentrate upon God.

St Benedict then sees these two realities in our life – prayer and community – as essentially one. Concentration upon our neighbour in love and on God in our prayer is for St Benedict the same sharing in the perpetual prayer of Christ which is his loving relationship with his Father. The monastery itself is based on and rooted in precisely this loving relationship.

In the monastic prayer of St Benedict's day this was perhaps more obvious when the community deepened its sense of its own transcendent character by periods of common silent worship in and after the Divine Office.

St Benedict's Rule does not give an ordered exposition of his theory of prayer. But he does unequivocally instruct his monks to pray often and to this end he sets apart a special room for prayer in the monastery which is a place of silence. All are to respect the especially reverential character of this room – the oratory. Prayer was to be short rather than long, frequent, simple and silent. 'Use tears rather than words', he tells us.

And yet with these few strokes of the brush the great master does highlight the highroad to Benedictine contemplation. Silence, reverence, purity of heart, mystery. The monk, by the general direction of his life, is becoming daily more sensitive to the presence of God. What could be more natural than to call frequently to mind the ineffable mystery of God's presence among us and to worship silently? The prayer room itself becomes a reminder to us to enter frequently into the chamber of our own heart, there to rejoice with the Lord.

But although Benedict doesn't himself write a full discourse on prayer he does refer the reader to Cassian. It might seem strange that so great a master as St Benedict gives so little precise instruction on prayer, and yet devotes so much attention to the petty minutiae of community living. The answer surely is that like so many spiritual masters before and since, St Benedict found it almost impossible to discourse at length on an experience he apprehended as truly ineffable. One of his instructions to his monks was not be fond of much talking.

When we turn to Cassian's *Conferences* which St Benedict clearly knew intimately we find a doctrine on prayer that is wholly consistent with everything we find in the Rule. Both Cassian and Benedict share the same fundamental view of monastic life. 'Above all', Cassian tells us in his first *Conference*, 'the end of our profession is the Kingdom of God. But the immediate aim is purity of heart without which no one can gain that end.'

This stress on the Kingdom of God is of tremendous importance for it points out the whole character of the monastic life so vividly. The concept of the Kingdom of God points to the absolute dominion of God in the life of the monk. The monk is the one who has been seized by God's Word: 'Listen, O son.' And indeed from this concept comes the whole notion of the prophetic character of monasticism. As a result of our listening, as a result of our own experience of that Kingdom – the dominion of God in our own hearts – the monk's very life proclaims the Kingdom of God, that 'Christ is all and is in all' (Col. 3:11). Herein lies the transforming power of the monastic life. The monk's life is a continuing summons to life by God's Word. Cassian uses the Synoptic Gospels' imagery of the Kingdom of God but he might just as well have used the Johannine image of 'life in all its fullness' for this is truly the end of our profession – fullness of life.

> As we progress in our monastic life and our faith, our heart expands and we run along the way of God's commands with a delight of love that cannot be described. (Prol. 49)

The way to purity of heart without which no one can gain the Kingdom is not without its difficulties and indeed the way to purity of heart might well be described as the art of the monastic life. And Benedict in the Prologue makes it very clear that he is addressing those 'who renounce their own wills'. He uses such expressions as 'forbidding their own wills', 'abandoning our wills', 'taking no pleasure in carrying out our own desire'. Then, with that marvellous range and ease of his authority he puts it quite simply in these words, 'It is not lawful for a monk to have either his body or his will at his own disposal.' And his summary of the character of the monk includes the same idea: 'They do not live by their own free will or obey their own desires and pleasures but walk by another's judgment and commands.'

St Benedict realized that purity of heart meant the capacity to turn wholly and utterly to the other. He realized with complete clarity that this in turn meant a turning away from self and he saw that turning from self meant the transcending of all desire. The life of the monk is beyond desire precisely because it is a life of intimate union with God. But this union of hearts is to be enjoyed only if there is a constant turning to the other, a constant conversion, a continuing purity of heart. Benedict realized that he had located the essence of the spiritual life in his quest for purity of heart. Cassian and the Egyptian Fathers went much further. They went on to talk of the killing, the mortification of the self. It is remarkable that though the words *mortificare* and *mortificatio* are frequently used by Cassian they are nowhere used by St Benedict. He realized that we should not have a negative aim of mortifying ourselves without the positive experience of our growth in virtue by concentrating in love on the other.

The renunciation of self-will that St Benedict envisages is not associated with a renunciation of the affections advocated by St John of the Cross, the great apostle of detachment a thousand years after St Benedict's time. John of the Cross wrote that for the spiritual person no joy or pleasure in anything, natural or spiritual, is permitted as 'there is nothing which a man may rejoice in except serving God'.

How differently St Benedict seeks to achieve the same end of unimpeded contemplation:

> The elder monks are to love the younger and the younger to obey the elder with all charity and all are to cherish fraternal love chastely as brothers.

We can sense in this wonderfully human vision of a truly loving community something of the warmth of the southern Italian sun. And so it is all the more remarkable that an Englishman like St Aelred of Rievaulx should have so thoroughly assimilated Benedict's spirit as to be able to incarnate his loving brotherhood in the more austere climes of Yorkshire. The thesis of his *De Amicitia Spirituale* is precisely that of exploring your relationship with God through human friendship. The way of perfection in St Benedict's vision, therefore, is never the way of rejection but always the way of transcendence. In the community we find the human context of transcendence and so also the context of prayer.

Saint Benedict: Leader as Hero

Every age and every people has called forth its leaders. The leader is a universal phenomenon of mankind as a social being. But there is more than one type of leader. Clearly, we have to make a fundamental distinction between Alexander the Great and a modern American president, or between St Benedict and an emotive evangelical preacher. The distinction I find useful separates leaders into one of two types: the hero and the father figure. I would see Alexander and St Benedict as heroes and most of the presidents and preachers as father figures. This distinction, as you will see, is not based on the ideas or methods the leaders use but rather on the scope of their vision – their vision of human nature and of their own age – and on the long-term consequences of their life among people.

I would like to develop this distinction a little. The hero, according to Jung, is an archetype we can find expressed in many of the myths and fairytales where the hero leaves family and friends to embark upon an adventure: either a quest or the slaying of a monster or the freeing of an innocent victim of evil. When he has succeeded in his mission, the hero is rewarded with a happy marriage and there, one might think, the tale should end. In our cinema and television fantasies constructed around this archetype this is indeed where it usually does end. And how often do we not feel a sense of incompletion? But in the full expression of the symbol, with the tasks of the first-half of his life completed the hero is killed or sacrifices himself: like Siegfried or the Egyptian Osiris. And then, the hero is resurrected. But rather than returning to earth as before, he reigns 'in a kingdom not of this world'. As one psychologist has written:

Perhaps the death of the hero could be taken as signifying a turning-point in life at which the ego has to relinquish the seat of power and acknowledge its dependence upon something or someone greater than itself.[2]

The hero, then, in his life and as often in his death, too, leads because he stimulates his fellow-people by his magnanimous vision, courage and example. He opens horizons. He develops initiatives. He develops creativity. He calls to adventure: to a share in the adventure he has discovered perhaps at the cost of his life. An adventure not without its dangers but not without its rewards either. It is not an adventure one simply undertakes but it is an adventure to which one is *summoned*. The leader as father figure is sometimes misinterpreted by his devotees as a hero despite the fact that real heroes do not encourage 'hero-worship'. The father figure protects where the hero explores and takes risks; he does the thinking for the society, shows it the safe paths to follow. The father figure knows 'enough' already, perhaps even knows it *all*, whereas the hero says, 'We have more to find out. The adventure is beginning.' The father figure counsels safety and moves along the tramlines of tradition.

The story of an anthropologist on field-work in Kenya in the Forties shows the point. He was investigating a particular tribe and was amazed to hear its members tell him they had no dreams. Later, he realized that they meant they attached no significance to their dreams. This also seemed strange until he found that it was the medicine-men who did the tribe's dreaming, foretelling their future and interpreting their social symbols. But when he approached the medicine-men he found they too had 'stopped dreaming'. 'How long have you stopped dreaming?' he asked them. And he was told, since the arrival of the British District Officer. The white man had become the tribe's father figure in place of the medicine-men because it was he who now took their decisions, shaped their future and protected them.

We should, however, be wary of thinking of the heroic leader as merely a mythic or primitive phenomenon. He is in fact

2. Anthony Storr, *Jung* (Glasgow, Collins Fontana, 1973), p. 84.

called forth by developed, not undeveloped consciousness: by the ancient Greeks, not by pre-war Germany. It is the barbarian, not the civilized person who is hidebound by his or her fears who seeks the comforting protection of the father figure.

St Benedict is a Father who is a heroic leader, civilized and developed. His leadership is incarnate in a Rule of life which he wrote for people who had chosen an adventure, even though one very different from the excitements and pleasures known to most people. The Rule is not a strident manifesto: its first word is 'listen' and it ends by saying 'you will get there, you'll make it'. This seems a modest statement of his role as leader and I think the modesty is genuine. Most people of genius have been aware that their work will live after them even if they are denied recognition in their lifetime and they write with an eye on posterity. But the Rule of St Benedict shows complete concentration on the present and this, of course, makes it timeless. It has the note of true realistic humility and it *has* lasted. For five centuries practically every important figure on the world-stage was brought up under the direct influence of the Rule. For five centuries the Rule was the best known work in the West apart from the Bible. It was the early inspiration of most of the founders of modern Europe, scholars and politicians: Augustine, Anselm, Lanfranc, Gregory the Great, Gregory VII, St Boniface who took Christianity to Germany and, in England, St Bede.

St Benedict, the man, and his Rule are one and the same entity for us, if only because we know so little about his life that is not legend and so little of himself that is not conveyed through his work. We know him through the Rule, not through history or legend although St Gregory, who wrote his life, gives us one illuminating insight into his character. Benedict could not abide the Roman schools of his day and shunned them, becoming as Gregory tells us,

Scienter nescius et sapienter indoctus
(deliberately ignorant and wisely uneducated).[3]

Like many another person of genius before and since, Benedict

3. St Gregory the Great, *Dialogues* (New York, Fathers of the Church, 1959), vol. 39, p. 56.

was able to transcend the cultural concepts of his own time because he had never had his brain washed or his spirit broken by an excellent education in them.

But, as I said, we know Benedict through the Rule and in a deep sense the Rule *is* St Benedict for us. It shows us him as a man of authority and whereas authoritarianism is a mark of the father figure, authority belongs to the heroic leader. As the Gospels tell us authority was universally acknowledged as belonging to Christ. When we listen to such a leader we do not hear merely a well-assembled series of brilliant epigrams. In the Rule we detect the unifying force of a central vision and every part of it points towards the centre. The inner coherence of the Rule explains its longevity. It has not died because it achieves reality. Other works have achieved this too but have not had so powerful an influence and this is because they lack what, to me, epitomizes the achievement of the Rule: the spirit of realistic compassion.

Benedict's authority is in equal proportion to his confidence in his judgment and this is best expressed in his opening words to the reader: 'Hearken, my son, to the commands of thy master.' But this natural self-assurance of the really heroic leader is not tied to a static, egotistic view of self. In the same chapter he continues: 'Let all follow the Rule as Master', showing us how closely the man and his message are identified. The man flows out of the narrow confines of his self into the universal relevance of his Rule and from the vantage of this extension of himself he speaks with *authority* – as the *author*. And, as we all know, if we are to be inspired to undertake a dangerous journey, if we are to extend our own frontiers, then we need someone of confidence and vision to state his or her wisdom and experience clearly and with authority.

The voice of the Rule is a voice of a free person who has gained freedom by transcendence of self. Nowhere is this freedom so excitingly proclaimed as in the vision of the community nature of the religious life. Here he is in the sixth century providing the wisdom for a workable participatory process for taking community decisions:

As often as any important business has to be done in the

monastery, let the abbot call together the whole community and himself set forth the matter . . . Now the reason why we have said all should be called to council, is that God often reveals what is better to the younger.[4]

Freedom to share life in this way can only be achieved by one who has transcended the self-protecting, anxious fears of the unrenewed self – and it can only be proclaimed by someone who has found Christian confidence in themselves. This is not essentially a confidence in personal talents or gifts. It is the confidence of one who has achieved the liberty to love others with total self-transcendence. St Benedict's authority is born of his loving-kindness, his concern for others, his selflessness, extraordinary generosity and largeness of heart. He has special words for the care and patience necessary with the very young, the old, delicate, sick and – even more wonderfully – with the ignorant, slow-moving and timid.

His self-confidence springs too from his unbounded confidence in the basic goodness of human nature and his conviction that a community based on mutual obedience, trust, acceptance and sensitivity will joyfully proclaim to the whole world what religion is really about. The community is unified by love. The abbot, he says, should desire to be loved rather than feared. Needless to say this community of love has a strong backbone: the abbot that emerges from the Rule is a picture of Benedict himself, a truly Roman integration of *imperium, gravitas, stabilitas, rationabilis* and *mensurate* . . . a formidable prototype for his successors to repeat.

The life of this community is seen in a three-fold aspect: common worship, study and work. And the purpose of this division is to emphasize the totality of the life of prayer and discipline which constitutes the monastic adventure and which aims to lead each monk to his full humanity and the monastery to a deeper and deepening Christian vitality. The Rule was the great turning-point in the monastic life because it lays down the reasonable and realistic foundations for a person's search for God within a framework where there would be wise teach-

4. J. McCann, *The Rule of St Benedict* (London, Sheed and Ward, 1976), p. 10.

ers who had made the journey ahead of the beginners and who would inspire them in their own particular quest. Again and again in the Rule we are reminded of the dangers of losing touch with reality or becoming an eccentric extremist. Again and again the order into which the life is shaped and the importance of fellowship and mutual love remind us that the object of the exercise is being more firmly grasped by reality, not losing touch with it. But in the maturity of his own realism St Benedict is consistently aware that, in the words of T.S. Eliot, 'Human kind cannot bear very much reality'[5] and that his capacity to bear more is increased by gentleness and not by force.

The Rule of St Benedict clearly has had great historical importance and even today it is a vital influence in the lives of many thousands. But it is no longer so widely influential at all levels of society. Does this mean that the Rule is relevant only to monks and nuns who live by it but whose contact with the non-monastic world is subject to an entirely different set of more 'pragmatic' principles?

To answer this question we must have some formed ideas of our own regarding the kind of society we help to compose. It has been called the 'post-industrial' society. But what does this mean? It means, I think, that the central focal points of our corporate concerns have shifted. In the 'pre-industrial' age these concerns were religion and nature. In other words, it was in terms of religion and nature that people asked questions and contrived the answers which allowed them to live together and achieve the stability necessary for progress. The industrial age itself ousted these concerns and instead people thought and acted in terms of the work-ethic and social respectability. Now in our own post-industrial society new focal points of concern are appearing and these are relationships and culture. These are the new terms in which we now phrase the essentially unchanging adventure of life. What both relationships and culture have in common is an assumption of the existence of and need for *community*. More than one relationship is, however embryonically, already 'community' and culture is a social

5. T. S. Eliot, 'East Coker', *Four Quartets*.

experience. We should not be fooled into dismissing these themes of our day just as ideas fostered by popular psychology and the media because the underlying assumption of the need for community is a very serious and urgent one. We are cease-lessly asking ourselves questions about community: what is its nature, is it affected by numbers of people or cultural diversity, how should it be governed, how do we get back to a real practical experience of it?

The unacknowledged boon of our times which prompts these questions and gives us time to ask them is *leisure*, which tech-nology has thrust upon us but which we have not yet learned to employ joyfully and creatively. Many people use their leisure in the search for community in the form of social organizations within society: hobby-clubs, protest groups, ratepayers' associ-ations, trade unions, professional bodies and political parties. Cohesion in society as a whole depends upon people working well together within such social units and depends equally, of course, upon the various groups working well together. But as we know it is possible to become self-conscious and partisan about one's membership of such a body at the expense of one's sense of belonging to the larger social unity. But whatever the dangers or disadvantages, the overall benefit of such bodies is inestimable. Even if they may fall short of satisfying our basic need for community, however much they may seem to create tension and rivalry rather than love and harmony, nevertheless it is true in most cases that the person who belongs to no group, no community, is infinitely worse off because, in a sense, he or she does not exist at all if not in relationship with others.

Most people have come to realize this and continue to be active in small specialized organizations. But there remains an unsatisfied desire for *complete* community, for the association with others that will not merely co-ordinate cultural or econ-omic aspirations but that will provide for the development of the individual on all levels and in his or her full potentiality. Such a community will express and incarnate the basic sense of identity as a human being, lovable and desirous of loving. There must, in other words, be a nexus of small social units which give a sense of total belonging, total acceptance and the integration of all these units enriches society as a whole.

St Benedict understood the nature of such community as his Rule testifies. The principles of such a monastic life are such as these.

Let everyone participate in the government.
Let everyone know he is an honoured member of society.
Look after all the more vulnerable members of society.
Have gentleness in all reforms.

These injunctions have a deep significance on the purely natural level of human association. But because they express the *truth* about community their significance is also transposed to the supernatural level. It is, of course, only too easy to make them sound facile or sentimental in our own days of post-industrial readjustment. Despite our recognition of our need for community we hardly know on what basis to begin building a social fraternity. Our ignorance and fear are largely attributable to the breakdown in confidence of the values of the preceding age of the industrial society. We can no longer shape our lives and relationships in terms of the work ethic or the maintenance of social respectability. We look out on a confused world where stability is not only threatened but has in many ways already been overthrown.

Perhaps St Benedict would have little relevance to us today had he not lived in an age strikingly similar to our own. In the sixth century the cohesive power and institutions of the Roman empire were crumbling both because of disunity from within and pressure from without. And Rome itself, together with the whole of the imperial 'establishment', was entering a phase of self-destructive moral decadence. Out of this crisis of chaos and disunity arose the Rule of St Benedict for monasteries: a statement of the real possibilities of sharing life in its essential goodness within an atmosphere of order and sanity. In our own very similar circumstances the phenomenon of communes, communities and kibbutzes has arisen in every part of the world. How these ventures will develop we cannot say. But that they call for and need the spirit of leadership is certain. I believe that spirit can still be found, humane, wise and practical, in St Benedict. His vision of growth in goodness in a loving community is an indestructible truth.

We are not called upon slavishly to imitate his practical example. That would be to forego our participation in his vision and merely to indulge ourselves in nostalgic hero-worship. The heroic leader calls his disciples, with words of encouragement, to follow where he leads so that he may call them friends, not servants.[6] We must recreate his vision in the terms suitable to the needs of our own time. This we do by responding creatively and zealously to our vocation as men and women called to freedom and to perfection. We have the responsibility of trying to point the way ahead for the generations who will follow us. And this we do by proclaiming Benedict's vision of humanity as possessing the infinite importance of a creature called to a destiny transcending his or her own personal limitations from within a community based on natural wisdom and supernatural confidence.

6. Jn. 15:15.

The Other-Centredness of Mary

Preface

A few weeks after arriving in Montreal where we had been invited to found a new Benedictine Community, John Main was asked to speak to a meeting of the Religious of Montreal. He spoke on the evening of 7 December 1977 and chose Mary as his theme.

His subject was one which has often been much entangled in sentimentality and theological confusion. He brought to it his own strong intelligence and theological balance. By interpreting the biblical figure of Mary in terms of her spiritual symbolism rather than of the religious images that subsequently accumulated around her, he has restored Mary to a place of universal contemporary value. He has shown how she witnesses to perennial features of the human journey of prayer and testifies to the fundamental conditions which make our spiritual pilgrimage possible.

In his thought and life John Main had a deep and abiding love of the sacred traditional ways. He had a profound and gentle sympathy for the simple faith. But he was uncompromising in his resistance to mere religiosity and superstition. He was never slow to recognize or point out the difference. Religion needed to be 'used sparingly', he would say, as it can be such a potent influence and can so easily suffocate the spiritual and the true. Mankind has such a strong tendency to prefer the sound of its own disputing voice to the silence of God.

In clearing away so much of the false religiosity that accumulates around our great religious symbols we restore them to their primal function, to point beyond themselves. This was always John Main's aim in writing or talking about God or our journey to him, to lead to the perimeter of silence where our

155

words and images are surrendered in that rich poverty of spirit
to which Mary so supremely testifies.

Laurence Freeman OSB

The Other-Centredness of Mary

Every age and every civilization has its own special angle of perception. All people at all times have been inspired and transformed by their contemplation of the one Reality, which is the same yesterday, today and for all time. But in their approach to that Reality – their approach to the condition of pure, selfless contemplation – they have each had their own form of language and symbolism, and they have each constructed their own means for the attempt to express the inexpressible. The flux of the great religious images throughout the history of even one culture can bewilder us, but we nevertheless still have the feeling that something remains constant beneath all the cultural variations. This constant is, of course, the essential meaning and value that the images strive to express in forms that people of the day can both understand and respond to.

The distinction between *image* and *symbol* is here fundamental to an intelligent religious response, if this response can serve as a base and support for spiritual growth. Whereas the *image* is fixed in meaning and limited to the currency of its own age, the *symbol* points beyond itself, through its own rich meaning, towards a still deeper and simpler reality that is greater than itself. To understand *images*, not to be controlled by them or limited by their restricted perspective, we must, then, have a firm grasp of the *symbol* from which they emerge. In the case of Mary, for example, we have to be detached from the countless number of images by which her essential, rich meaning has found expression in Western Christendom. If we are, then we can approach the great symbolic meaning that the gospel bestows on her: a meaning that points beyond itself to Jesus. Just as the purpose of the great religious symbols is to lead us to the condition of pure prayer beyond images and concepts, so Mary's purpose and meaning is to lead us to Jesus who is the Word of God beyond language, whose name is the name above every other name.

The significance of Mary undergoes subtle shifts of meaning and relevance the more deeply she is understood, which is to say, the more clearly we see her within the total context of the gospel's teaching on the human vocation to holiness. Whereas Jesus is the Word that proceeds directly out of the creative silence of the Father, the Word which contains all meaning and all power, Mary is like a word echoing this supreme Logos: a word that grows out of the Word. Like a word in any language, Mary is apprehended under different meanings in different contexts and different ages. If in the past she has been accredited with an importance that seemed to rival or, in practice, surpass the central and unique importance of Jesus, it was often because some people seemed to have understood that her meaning was tied directly to that of Jesus – so intimately connected to it that the edges sometimes seemed blurred and a confusion of identity, common in every human mythology, would then begin to occur.

We, in our generation, have to be clear in our own minds what Mary's meaning is to us, and so we have to see her in the focus of her gospel context. Of course, the gospel is a living force in the present, not a 'golden age' of the past, and in the stream of the Christian tradition a great enrichment of its meaning takes place each time it is 'rediscovered' and 'realized' by individuals or by whole generations. So Mary's meaning for us will be one that has grown out of all the levels and interpenetrating streams of meaning with which she has been endowed in past centuries. These meanings cannot be erased – but nor can they be deep-frozen by romantic piety and preserved without change. The significance of any word, of any symbol, is the sum of its past meanings and its present context.

In the primitive Church Mary became for some the Christian expression and counterpart of the pagan fertility goddesses. To the Middle Ages she became the benevolent intermediary between God and his people, the protector of cities and of town guilds, the patroness of armies and Crusades: as it were a Christian Athene. We can understand and respect these meanings. And, as with our relation to tradition in general, we have to allow for the difference of a pre-Freudian mentality, more emotional, less self-critical, perhaps less self-aware and certainly less self-conscious a civilization than our own. But we cannot rest content with these outworn meanings or with the coolness of mere historical objectivity. We may know, for example, and benefit from knowing, that the word 'enthusiasm' once meant to be 'filled with godliness' but we cannot use the word seriously or relevantly with that as its principal meaning today. Yet it *is* part of its meaning today. The task is not merely to analyze and etymologize but to discover the fullness of contemporary meaning and relevance.

Mary does then most certainly have a significance for us – precisely because she is a part of the gospel and a central part of the first section of Luke's account of our salvation. To understand her meaning for us, we have to know the meanings she had in the past and we have to know what angle of perception predominates in our own day: what need her symbolic richness will answer for us.

In his preface to *Via Media*, Cardinal Newman spoke of the Church as a dynamic integration of the prophetic, the priestly and the kingly – that is, she expresses, she consecrates and she directs the way of human beings to God. But, he says, because the Church is so comprehensively relevant to people, their life and their thought, we have to distinguish between those areas in which the Church is an agent of revelation and where she is a force of evocation. In his own words:

> It must be recollected that while the Catholic Church is ever most precise in her enunciation of doctrine, her tone is different in the sanctions she gives to devotions, as they are of a subjective and personal nature.[1]

The vitality of Newman's vision of the Church was that he saw so clearly that Christianity was a 'universal religion, suited not simply to one locality or period, but all times and places'. And

1. *Via Media* (London and New York, Longmans, Green), vol. 1, Preface to 3rd edn.

because of its very universalism it is bound to 'vary in its relations and dealings towards the world around it; that is, it will develop'.[2]

For the majority of Christians it is the 'devotions' of which Newman speaks that are the principal experience of their religious response. It is because they are so 'subjective and personal' that we have to find a devotional life suitable for each successive age. Let us be clear, however, that the central purpose of all devotion is to propel us into the personal experience of transcendence in the power of the mystery – and this experience is our awareness of the indwelling Spirit of God living out the life of the most holy Trinity in our hearts. The importance of Mary and of Marian devotion is that her life has taken on an important symbolic significance in the Christian tradition and, by grasping this significance, we can experience ourselves as being real participants in the mystery of existence. Her place in the economy of salvation makes that economy more understandable – more human – for us. The harmony and holiness she radiates in the pages of Luke's Gospel help us forward to the same harmony and wholeness which arise from faithfulness, simplicity and self-transcendence.

In the rich tradition of Christian devotion, the figure of Mary stands out among all the 'devotions' of the Church as one of the richest and most personally identifiable signs of the real possibility of human harmony. All the aspects of the human spirit and its relationship with the corporeal dimension of our life find their fusion and perfect balance in Mary: her purity, her fertility and motherhood, her strength and humility. It is just this balance, this inner harmony of our human spirit and our human faculties that is the condition for prayer – and, in a real sense, too, the condition *of* prayer. It is this condition of prayer which leads to that full and undistorted awareness of our union with the Spirit of Jesus that the early Church Fathers knew and called the 'real knowledge of God' – conversion, the 'enlightenment of the eye of the heart'.

We do not tread the path of prayer alone – although we have

2. *An Essay on the Development of Christian Doctrine* (London and New York, Longmans, Green), ch. 2, sect. 1.

to enter into our own solitude. Nor do we tread it without signs that direct our pilgrimage or persons who help us to recognize and follow those signs. But to see the signs and to listen to the persons we need what Cardinal Newman called 'clear heads and open hearts'.

We have to approach Mary as one of the important gospel signs of our pilgrimage of prayer – and to make the approach without fuddled heads and merely pietistic hearts. To approach her in the mist of our own sentimentality is to objectify her – to make her an image or even an idol rather than a symbol. To apprehend her full meaning which expresses the breadth, the fullness and the tenderness of the Christian mystery, we will have to understand her as a person. Like everything that leads to fulfilment in Jesus, our understanding must itself be personal; that is, we must understand the gospel, the Word of God, as a personal communication opening up and exploring the depths of our own intimate personhood. The experience of prayer is the experience of being *known* – the prerequisite for the experience is to let go of our egotistic efforts to *know* which too often means to control and objectify. Such efforts invariably lead us into sterility and frustration. A traditional word for the necessary disposition for prayer, which the gospel incarnates in Luke's account of the Annunciation, is 'modesty'. There is no fear in modesty – which must be distinguished from shyness which *is* fearful. True modesty, where we allow the knowing-power of another to enter and explore us, is that readiness, openness and sensitivity we often call 'humility'.

Humility is the power that reveals and roots us in our precise place in relationship to another. As such, it is the basis of all real encounter. It is closely linked to another precondition for any personal encounter or relationship: a degree of detachment, a space which allows for the free play of the creative energy of love to effect union between us and the other. The space is usually filled with our own self-consciousness but in prayer it is emptied of all egoism and is filled instead with the pure consciousness of union in the power of love. Prayer itself is our awareness of our liberating union with the creative power of love that creates and sustains us in the person of Jesus. Because of the Incarnation, the tangible actuality of Jesus as

God and man – our brother – this awareness is something more than rational knowledge. We can talk intelligently, beautifully, usefully, of the Incarnation, but this is not in itself *knowing* the person of Jesus as a living reality in and of my being. We can spend a lifetime studying the work and personality of Charlemagne or Bismarck but this is not really knowing them – and can never be because no personal, living link unites them to us any more. In the case of Jesus we have this link in his Spirit which fills our inmost being with the infinite, loving power of his resurrected life. And so we can *know* the person of Jesus but it is with the 'real knowledge' or 'full knowledge' spoken of by St Paul when he exhorted the Church to know the love of Christ 'though it is beyond knowledge'.

This is knowledge in the Hebraic sense, a relationship of love in full, creative and mutually liberating union which transcends the objectifying and distorting prism of self-consciousness. In prayer, in allowing the prayer of Jesus to expand and rise unfettered within us, we are deepening our awareness of such a union already realized. And we deepen it at a level of our being – of our personhood – which centralizes and focuses all our powers and all the aspects of our consciousness. In prayer we are known, and as a result we know with the knowledge by which we are known because our spirit becomes one with the Spirit of God. The fulfilment of this mystery is retarded if we act as though we need to know that we know – if we try to 'experience the experience'. In prayer we are led into the full and simple experience, the *ecstasis* beyond our self-consciousness, beyond our conceptual limitations, beyond the vanity of the imagination and the hubris of the intellect. It was from this experience of wholly undifferentiated union and perfect harmony of consciousness that the first monks of the fourth and fifth centuries arrived at the definition of true prayer as the prayer wherein the monk does not know that he is praying.

This can seem to our cerebral conceptualization of prayer as a definition of mere oblivion, a mind-blown state. And, indeed, from the middle ground of language between the silence of oblivion and the silence of full consciousness, the two states are not easily differentiated in words or images. But the difference between the two silences – the unselfconsciousness of the prayer-full state and the vacuum of non-being – is, quite literally, the difference between life and death. What brings us out of the dead silence to the living, conscious silence which leads us into the knowledge of our union with God is the Word, made living and active by the power of the Spirit praying in our heart. The personal experience of this power is the goal of the Christian pilgrimage of prayer. As we follow the pilgrimage we grow into an ever deeper simplicity, an ever sharper and more immediate encounter. We come less and less to seek to 'experience the experience' but rather to allow the experience to be, to emerge, to expand and to transform us.

From the earliest years of the Christian era it was realized that the figure of Mary expressed the subtle – and mysteriously simple – blend of elements that makes it possible to persevere on the pilgrimage of prayer. The Fathers saw this so clearly and saw their own experience of the pilgrimage so well reflected in the person of Mary emerging in the Christian thought of their period that they were sometimes led to allegorize Mary out of any approachable, personal value. She became too often just an allegorical value for a writer's favourite virtue. It is true, of course, that the Christian meaning of Mary is essentially symbolic but this is a far richer and more comprehensive quality than the allegorical. We all have symbolic value as persons, both from within our own psyche, in our relationship with ourselves, and also in our encounters and deeper relationships with others. At both these levels our symbolic value is something beyond the realm of merely rational investigation. But the symbolic is nonetheless an essential function of the personal. And because Christianity is, par excellence, the realm of the fully personal it is characterized by a rich and expressive symbolism.

To say, therefore, that Mary has a symbolic meaning in Luke's Gospel, the most literary and sophisticated of the synoptics, is not merely to say that there is an evident symbolic identification of Mary with the long line of holy women from the Old Testament. (It is of academic rather than personal importance that the Magnificat is derived from the Song of Hannah.) The real meaning of Mary as an expression, a

163

symbol, of human holiness is to be found rather in the direct relevance she was meant to have for the Christian readers or listeners of the gospel – who were already on their pilgrimage and intent upon the purification of their intention and the deepening of their commitment.

From this relevance to the ordinary Christian on the pilgrimage of prayer there developed in later Christian thought the identification of Mary both with the individual human spirit and with the Church as both of these are involved in the continuing process of redemption. The essence of this identification is likewise the secret of Mary's universal appeal, also to us of the twentieth century; that secret is her interiority.

This brings me to my starting point. Every age has its particular angle of perception; that is to say, it is characterized by a particular concern and feels this as a particular need more deeply than others. To an era perhaps concerned with survival and multiplication, Mary could best be apprehended through her creativity, her fertility, her place in the archetypal cycle of death and rebirth. To an era of violent insecurity she would become the symbol of protection and maternal solicitude. To our own era, intent upon a rediscovery of an inner life that has been largely dissipated in materialistic systems of thought and of society, an age seeking for an affirmation of the reality of the spiritual dimension in human beings, Mary is above all the symbol of a rich, healthy and creative interiority.

The confusion we tend to make in the West is between Mary's motherhood and her interiority. We have emphasized the attractive, consoling mother out of proportion to the God-centred spirit of prayer, her 'other-centredness'.

As Mother she will, of course, always have powerful psychological and symbolic value. The psychoanalyst explains her cult as the answer to a person's yearning for the pure mother who will never let him or her down. Because this side of Mary's many-faceted meaning has tended to predominate under the influence of Augustinian morality, her importance in the realm of sexual symbolism has been exaggerated. Much more was written in *defence* of her virginity than in *proclamation* of her importance as a model for prayer, and this because she became enmeshed, in unclear minds, with a particular society's under-standing, or misunderstanding, of human sexuality.

Mary is one of the greatest expressions in any culture of the wholly fulfilled woman, complete in her motherhood, her womanhood, and complete, too, in her spiritual maturity. And because both were complete there is no real demarcation between them. In Mary, as in Jesus, we see the expression of the essential correspondence between body and spirit which itself finds expression in the New Testament account of the Ascension and, later, in the Assumption. The importance of these accounts is that they remind us of the integration of the whole person in the Christian mystery and the continuity of this integration in the fulfilled life of the Resurrection.

And so, within her gospel meaning, which is the criterion by which all understanding of Mary should be evaluated, Mary's motherhood is a sign, a sacrament of her full interiority. If Mary became so valuable a symbol of prayer for the early Church Fathers it was because they were inspired by their own experience of the interiority of the Christian mystery. In Mary they saw a reflection, indeed the ideal, of their own experience. They responded so warmly to Mary, the mother of Jesus, because they knew that every Christian is called to bring Jesus to birth within him or her; that, as Jesus was conceived and grew in bodily reality within Mary, so no less really he is conceived by the power of the Spirit and grows to full stature with the power of love within every responsive human heart. Just as the essential condition for Mary's reception of Jesus was her openness and her simplicity – what the gospel calls 'purity of heart' – so also, purity of heart is necessary for every Christian.

All Christians are invited to discover within their inmost being a force of love, a light, a personal presence infinitely greater than themselves – and to *know* it. As Jesus himself grew more fully to know his own personhood, in his love of his Father, so also Mary grew in understanding of the person who entered the world of human beings through her. In chapter 2 of his Gospel Luke tells us that Mary failed to understand what the child Jesus meant when he spoke of his mission among people. In chapter 19 of John's Gospel her now mature understanding is expressed in the silence in which she stands at the foot of the cross. In the same way, all Christians on the pilgrimage of prayer come to know more clearly and more deeply the meaning of the love that floods their inmost heart when they turn away from themselves toward the Lord. Their knowledge deepens and so does the silence within them from which the knowledge grows. They, too, learn to worship in silence.

For Mary, the fruit of her openness to the Spirit of God was her loving relationship with a living child. In the higher order of reality to which the life, death and resurrection of that child has called us, the fruit of our openness to the Spirit is our loving relationship with the living God. In that relationship we discover our own true selfhood: we uncover our own Godlike potential. The Christian vocation is to know ourselves in the Spirit of Jesus. This is the knowledge that leads us to see our union with all our brothers and sisters in the redemptive love of Jesus.

The presence of Mary in the gospel is an eloquent and economical description of the means by which we come to this post-Resurrection knowledge, the realization and 'second birth' of which Jesus spoke. It was the essence of the vitality of the early Church that it understood from such a depth of personal knowledge the real meaning of 'purity of heart' and knew it as the fruit of 'poverty of spirit'. Because it was understood with such clarity and immediacy it could be proclaimed with courage and authority. They understood poverty of spirit as that condition of other-centredness in the human spirit which allows it to realize, become aware of its union with the Lord Jesus. The term came, therefore, to be almost synonymous with the condition of prayer. John Cassian, St Benedict's teacher of prayer, talks of prayer as the attainment of 'grand poverty' by means of the purification of meditation.

Without the bedrock experience of the living presence of the Spirit in our heart, the spiritual life dies, its systems and forms atrophying. The poverty of spirit to which our pilgrimage calls us is not self-imposed or the creation of our own self-aggrandizement. It is the inevitable corollary of turning the searchlight of consciousness off ourselves and onto the Other – the Lord dwelling within us. This is the essential Christian insight which Mary exemplifies in Luke's Gospel: a poverty of spirit that is itself a purity of heart because it is unsullied by the intrusion of the egotistic will seeking for experience, desiring holiness, objectifying the Spirit or creating God in its own image. Mary reveals the basic simplicity of the Christian response in a poverty of spirit that consists in turning wholly to God, wholly away from self.

Mary is the perfect type of the human spirit *persevering* in faith and love on the way of openness and receptivity. Her own life history, such as we can follow it in the gospel narrative, points up the essence of the pilgrimage of prayer and expresses the growth of the spirit on its pilgrimage. Her qualities exemplify the necessary dispositions of mind and heart as we attend to the indwelling mystery of Christ's presence. As Merton put it:

> The geographical pilgrimage is the symbolic acting out of an inner journey. The inner journey is the interpolation of the meanings and signs of the outer pilgrimage.[3]

That is a concise account of the way Mary's role in the gospel relates to the personal pilgrimage of every one of us. The meaning and sign of Mary's historical journey is also summed up in her central experience of detachment, the quality that necessarily characterizes the condition of the person for the path of prayer.

Firstly, there is the detachment from any obstructive view of self: what I am, what I am doing, what I am achieving, what degree of perfection I have reached today. Mary exemplifies a person in his or her most natural condition before an image of self complicates and distorts: a condition of 'complete simplicity demanding not less than everything' as Julian of Norwich put it. Mary does not have an image of herself and an image of God. She wastes no spiritual energy in maintaining such a double vision and false antinomy. In receiving the news of her being chosen to bear the Messiah of her people, her response is immediately and naturally directed wholly to God. She is not unaware of the momentousness of the event, but she knows it

3. 'Pilgrimage and Crusade' in *Mystics and Zen Masters* (New York, Delta Books, 1967), p. 92.

simply, directly rather than self-consciously. She is not looking at herself having the experience. The very translucency of her knowledge is itself her fertility, the purity of her consciousness is the transcendent virginity of her spirit. A medieval English carol captures the medium of the Incarnation:

> He came all so stille
> To his mother's bower
> As dew in April
> That falleth on the flower.[4]

Detachment is only the counterpart to concentration. Any decision *for* something must also be a decision against or transcendence of something else. In Mary's gospel response, as in the dynamic of prayer, the condition of detachment is really a concentration upon the Reality that contains and perfects all things. In removing ourselves from the shadow of things, we in fact affirm and receive their real substance. In turning away from our ego, the shadowy, distracted, desiring ego, we in fact discover and enter into free possession of our true self. Similarly, Mary received a fulfilment of being that, in the words of St Paul, was the 'fullness of God himself'.

One of the first consequences of spiritual detachment is the liberation of the medium of *creative silence* – the condition of prayer in which we turn away from the noisiness of our own mind and turn towards the full silence of God. We become adapted to silence and wait, in faith, for the utterance of his Word within us which is the occasion of our second birth, our realization. Mary is characterized by such silence in the Gospels. In Matthew's she does not speak at all. In Luke's account she speaks four times, on each occasion testifying to the complete receptivity of her Spirit to the power of God and to the silent one-pointedness of its concentration on God. Even at times of doubt or confusion in the face of her son's growth and development, her response is essentially one of silence: a silence centred and concentrated, patient and hopeful: 'His mother treasured up all these things in her heart.'[5]

4. *Medieval English Lyrics*, ed. R.T. Davies (London, Faber and Faber, 1963), p. 155.
5. Lk. 2:51.

Her silence possesses a radiant creativity and consciousness because it is so clearly the positive, affirmative silence of other-centredness. She is not retreating from reality into a private netherworld but is attendant upon the emergence of the grand design of her life and the full revelation of its meaning. Her transcendence of self is the archetypal other-centredness of a mother's love for her child: a relationship that captured the Jewish religious imagination long before, both as an expression of God's unfailing love for human beings and of their dependence on God. The reality of such a relationship is only revealed in silence. And it is only in silence and through silence that we can interiorize what is beyond our comprehension and apprehend the power of a design larger than ourselves: it is the medium of *transcendence*.

If the prospect of this experience frightens us, it is often because we think that it will involve a kind of dehumanization of ourselves, that silence will isolate us from our fellow human beings. Mary is a sign that this is the false fear of an ego defending itself against reality. We encounter Mary in the gospel as a personal symbol – as a real human being who has entered upon the pilgrimage of love and been led into a state of consciousness, of purity of heart, that allows the energies and qualities of the human spirit to shine forth with unusual radiance. The important thing for us to realize is that she is human and, precisely because she is a fully developed person, she testifies to a reality that the unenlightened spirit cannot enjoy.

The condition of her 'complete simplicity' is the fruit of a paradox entered into by a spirit in silent *equilibrium*. She accepted the creative tensions of life with openness and alertness, and her simplicity is therefore neither naïve nor escapist. The figure of Mary has appealed to the religious consciousness so deeply because she reflects these paradoxes as creative experiences which have meaning beyond themselves. The joy and suffering of her life opened up the depths of her spirit to the knowledge of God's infinite goodness and compassion. Among the traditions of Western art, two of the most deeply imbedded images are those of the rapturous, fulfilled *madonna* and the grief-stricken *mater dolorosa*, testifying to the necessity of both these extremes of experience and suggesting, in the

169

greatest art, the ultimate transcendence. Throughout the paradox, however, the figure of Mary remains stable and balanced. The gospel suggests the silent depth of her perception in faith and reveals her perseverance in faith, undistracted by either extreme of emotional experience because the centre of her consciousness is not herself but Jesus. She is, therefore, the living exemplar of one rooted and founded in Christ. And it is her other-centredness that makes her our model for prayer.

At the core of Mary's detachment, even from what is dearest and most precious, is the continual projection of her consciousness away from herself. This is indeed the condition of her pilgrimage. On every occasion where Jesus is shown addressing her in the Gospel a further degree of detachment is achieved. In the Temple, at Cana, when the crowd drew Jesus' attention to her, Mary is each time confronted with the hard truth of the path of prayer that 'the way of possession is the way of dispossession'. No mother has ever possessed her son less possessively than Mary and for that reason none has been able to be as open to his experience. The whole of Mary's life is presented as a silent and loving response to the progressive detachment of her spirit. She stands before the mystery of her own life as before the mystery of God with ever-increasing simplicity, deepening vulnerability and an ever more refined sensitivity to the transforming power of love.

As an expression of the possibility of truly human holiness, Mary is a figure of universal relevance. Many non-Christian religions have apprehended her significance in the religious quest of human beings as a sign of the secret of that inner response that opens the heart to the indwelling spirit. Many of the iconographers of the gospel have seen the Mary who stands at the foot of the cross as a summation of the ancient female symbols that expressed the deeply involved feelings of a people about death and fertility. In her mourning she propitiates those same forces of sterility that the sacrifice of Jesus appeases. Where he is the sacrificial offering, she represents the principle of the abiding earth. Similarly, the virginity of Mary as it was understood in later Christian thought recalls the perpetual virginity of a Hera. Many a Hindu temple and ashram around the world will give prominent place to a statue or picture of Mary.

What these things suggest is not the mere relativity of Christian experience but rather its universality and comprehensiveness. Jesus did not live and teach in a cultural vacuum. He absorbed the accumulated and often derivative wisdom of his native culture and made use of the resources of its symbolism and language. In the same way, his continuing presence in the Church guarantees that he will never become identified with one particular culture, one particular form of worship or organization. The Christian experience of the indwelling Spirit of the risen Lord is the summation and fulfilment of all humanity's spiritual longing and experience. The rich texture of symbolism and myth that the Church adopted from humanity's common religious heritage and adapted to its own refined intuitions and fuller experience points up to the expansion of the Christian experience, not its localization. And in the progressive revelation of the mystery of his risen life we are seeing more clearly that the focus of all human awareness of God in every culture is the person of Jesus, his Son, our brother:

> In him everything in heaven and on earth was created, things visible and invisible . . . He is before all else that is. In him everything continues in being. It pleased God to make absolute fullness reside in him and by means of him to reconcile everything in his person.[6]

The universality of Mary's spiritual relevance should not, then, disquiet us as much as remind us of the universality of Christianity, which is to say the universal presence and power of Jesus. Similarly, the multifacetedness of her meaning serves to show the centrality of the Christian experience in relation to all the levels of the human spirit. To a Jungian psychoanalyst, for example, Mary is the expression of the *anima* in human beings, the guiding spirit that leads the whole person to fullness on the path of individuation. Or, in Chinese philosophy, she is identified with *Yin*, the feminine principle that imbues us with sensitivity, intuition, reverence. It is, then, in her femininity that her association with the human spirit becomes most understandable.

6. Col. 1:16ff; see Eph. 1:10.

The Mary of the gospel expresses the fruit of inner harmony, the fruit of integration and balance. Later reflection on this elaborated and sophisticated Mary. But the essential value of her meaning is constant when she is seen to point to the necessity of silence and other-centredness for the pilgrimage of prayer.

The most powerful aspect of her meaning for people today, however, is the need for a true inner harmony as the foundation of the pilgrimage. She shows the need for the resolution of the dissonant faculties in us, the transcendence of our sense of duality in relation to ourself and to God, the integration of *Yin* and *Yang*, the concentration of our spirit upon the source of our being. This has been the perennial Christian insight into prayer. The way to realize the fusion of our spirit with the spirit of the risen, universal Jesus is to allow the Holy Spirit to work freely, rise transcendentally in our heart where he has come to dwell in love. This realization is the path of prayer and it requires openness and perseverance in openness to the whole wonder of our creation and redemption.

> I tell you the truth when I say that this work demands great serenity and an integrated and pure disposition in soul and body . . . God forbid that I should separate what God has coupled, the body and the spirit . . . Indeed we owe God the homage of our whole person, body and spirit together. And, fittingly enough, he will glorify our whole person, body and spirit, in eternity.[7]

This is an enlightened description of prayer that has sprung from the depth of an experience that reveals prayer as wholly personal and as the most natural activity of the human spirit, the state of being for which we were created. We can tell it is enlightened because it proclaims life in its fullness – the full life which Jesus preached and now communicates to us through his indwelling Spirit. The radiant figure of Mary in the gospel shows us that fullness in *fully human form*. We see in her the serenity, the integration and the pure disposition of which the *Cloud* speaks. We see, too, the fruit of this fullness which for us, as for her, is the birth of Jesus in our heart.

7. *Cloud of Unknowing*, tr. C. Wolters (Harmondsworth, Penguin Books, 1967), chs. 41 and 48.

Death – The Inner Journey

Preface

The last months of John Main's life form a model of his whole life. Throughout these months he continued to serve, teach and inspire with all the energy of his generous self-giving. Even when it was difficult for him to talk he taught by silence and by the spiritual power of his presence, a power that was always deepening. A living picture of the vitality and generosity that characterize even this last phase of his life makes a fitting introduction to this talk on death which was his last major public address.

On 12 May 1982 John Main began to suffer severe back pain which laid him up for several days. Although it was worse than usual we thought it was a recurrence of an old war injury. The pain eased after a while and he went to England and Ireland for two weeks of talks and retreats. It was a physically very demanding schedule and he was more than usually tired by it but gave of himself generously and unshrinkingly as he always did. Those who heard him speak and who meditated with him during these meetings were more than ever aware of the power of the peace that filled him and passed into those who were with him. He returned to Montreal and during the first week of July he and I gave retreats in Nova Scotia. Afterwards the rest of the Montreal Community came out to join us and we all spent a most idyllic two weeks in a house lent to us in Iona, a small village on the Bras d'Or Lakes.

Our daily routine there was a simple and regular one in which we meditated four times during the day. The day began with an early morning walk down to the sea and back for meditation and morning prayer. In the mornings he read or wrote, unless the children of a young family who were with us called him out for an early game of croquet or came in to talk to him asking for stories of his life. As always John Main brought a spirit of fun and enthusiasm to the simplest or most domestic undertaking. His back was giving him hardly any problems and the peaceful but lively days in the sun by the sea seemed to be restoring him to his usual health and vigour.

However on the journey home the pain returned and a period of suffering began that lasted until shortly before his death on 30 December. On the very night we returned to Montreal John Main was called to the bedside of an oblate of the community who was dying in the Palliative Care Unit of the Royal Victoria Hospital. He responded unhesitatingly. During the next weeks a period of diagnosis and treatment unfolded which only gradually made us aware of how critical his condition was. But whenever he was able to he gave himself generously to others, teaching more and more by his presence as well as by his words. On the evening of 18 November despite growing pain and weakness he went to talk to the Priory's oblate and meditation groups in Montreal meeting at the Villa Ste. Marguerite. This was his last meeting outside the monastery.

On 6 October he delivered this talk to two thousand delegates at the International Seminar on Terminal Care in Montreal. It is a unique chapter in his teaching on meditation written and spoken during a time of physical suffering when the awareness of his own approaching death was growing daily sharper. It was written with a specific audience in mind, those who care for the dying, and yet like all his teaching it is addressed to everyone. We all must die and, as John Main often said, we must learn how to die well.

Being with him in his own last days was to lose one's fear of death and to gain a sense of awe and reverence in its presence. To read his words printed here inspires in the same way. John Main was the most lively and life-loving of human beings. He never lost his sense of humour or sense of wonder at the mystery of life through all his final sufferings. But even in the best of health he was always clearly conscious of the mortality of time and he was as ready to die the next day as in ten years. This optimism and realism were rooted in the joy of the reality of God that he discovered in meditation. Generous in everything, he devoted his life to teaching and sharing the Christian tradition of meditation out of the authority of his own experience. He taught with his life and so also by his dying. Therefore his teaching lives.

Laurence Freeman OSB

Death – The Inner Journey

The person who would find his life must lose it.[1]
A paradox is a frightening reality to confront because we are
faced with two equally true forces each contradicting the other
and yet holding each other in place. The temptation is to ignore
one or the other. But if we ignore death we opt for a life of
superficiality and indeed fantasy. If on the other hand we ignore
life we go for an existence based on negativity and despair. We
have to find what both St Benedict and the Buddha called 'the
middle way'. We have to find the centre, the fulcrum or balanc-
ing point where we can allow the paradox simply to *be* in all
its dynamism and undefinability. We have to be able to find
this centre and to remain in it and to allow the energy flowing
between the poles of the paradox to pass through us, filling us
with energy and dynamism – and making us real.

I speak to you from the monastic tradition, in particular from
the Benedictine tradition. And from this Christian perspective
we see the centre as our own centre, our own heart. *The
Kingdom of Heaven is within you.*[2] To face death with a hope
that makes us fully human and to live with a spirit of liberty
and joy in being we must find this centre in time. We must
learn to be one with this centre, which is another way of saying
we must find our real selves. The search in our tradition is
conducted in stillness, in silence and with discipline. The search
is not in the first place an elaboration of concepts. It is not in
the first place an intellectual penetration of the mystery. In the
first place the search is conducted simply by allowing ourselves
to be.

1. Mt. 10:39.
2. Lk. 17:21.

The inner journey is a way of union. Firstly, it unites us to ourselves. Then (as our personal fulfilment is found beyond ourselves) it unites us to others. And then (as union with others opens up the heart of the mystery of love to us) it unites us with God, so that God may be all in all.[3]

False consolations and self-deceptions can hardly survive the process of dying to egoism. Death is the most immediate and overwhelmingly individual practicality we can experience. We have to prepare for our second death, the death of the body, by a way that is equally individual and practical and universal. It has to be a way that involves the whole self and this way of dying to the ego, the first death, is what we call prayer – the journey to our innermost centre. The journey beyond our own limitations.

It is important to remember never to separate death from life. If this inner journey is a death to egoism it is to the same degree a birth into life. But here as we elaborate the theory we must remember how utterly ordinary, how natural and obvious this process is, how real and how untheoretical.

Firstly, to grasp the naturalness of this journey we have to realize how practical it is. The way of making the journey to the fulcrum of the paradox, to the centre, is a way that has been trodden by men and women of the Spirit in every generation. The tradition of meditation in our monastic order is an ancient one, older than any institutional monasticism and rooted in the teachings of Jesus and the Judaic tradition that formed his human consciousness. The early monks were extraordinary men. They possessed a burning integrity, an absolute commitment allied to a gentle, sane and moderate humanity. They saw their spiritual life as inseparable from their ordinary life. They were neither spiritual egoists or spiritual materialists. They saw the way of meditation as a daily commitment to reality renewed and deepened every day.

It seems to me that if today we are as alienated as we are from the spiritual experience that gives meaning to life and death, it is because we have become alienated from the tradition that communicates the way to this experience. The teach-

3. 1 Cor. 15:28.

ing of the ancients was entirely practical. To make the inner journey you have to accept a daily discipline. To meditate you must set aside two periods, morning and evening of about half an hour each. And this time of meditation is not a time for thought or analysis or planning or introspection. It must be a time for silence, for stillness, for utter simplicity.

You sit down, you sit still, and the only essential rule of posture is to keep your back straight. It is important to be at the same time relaxed and alert. Lightly close your eyes and then silently, interiorly, begin to recite a single word or phrase, a word sacred in your own tradition but which, in so far as is possible, has no immediate verbal or conceptual associations. This word is widely called today a *mantra*. Learning to meditate is learning to say the mantra with fidelity and humility from the beginning of the period of your meditation until the end of it. We recommend to people beginning to meditate with us the word *maranatha* (an Aramaic word meaning 'Come Lord'). You should say the word continuously for the time of your meditation and if you find that distractions have taken you away from saying it, return to it and begin saying it again. Say it for the full time of your meditation, gently, humbly and lovingly.

The children who come to our monastery to meditate are a marvellous witness of the naturalness of this way of meditation. They are a real example for the adults who come. They show the essentially childlike quality that we need to tread the way. *Unless you become like little children you cannot enter the Kingdom of Heaven.*[4] It is a simple way. Its simplicity is its great challenge to us because we are trained to seek the truth, for accuracy, only in complexity. It is a *simple* but not necessarily *easy* way. It requires trust and perhaps indeed a certain recklessness to begin and it requires courage to persevere but all we have to lose are our own limitations.

This way, as I have suggested, is a way of dying *and* a way of living. While you are saying the mantra you are dying to what is the most difficult thing in the world for us to die to. We die to our own egoism, to our own self-centredness as we

4. Mk. 10:15.

181

go beyond our self-consciousness. And the reason is simply that while you are saying the mantra you are not thinking about yourself. You are attending to the mantra. And as through a lifetime you learn to say the mantra with deeper and deeper abandonment, with stronger and stronger faith, you die to everything that restrains you from the fullness of life. It is this fullness of life that is our destiny. As Jesus put it, *I have come that you may have life, life in all its fullness.*[5] As we die to the ego we rise to a way of life that astonishes us with its infinite richness, its wonder and, above all, with its absolute liberty of spirit. Meditation is a healing process. What is healed is the essential wound we all have: the wound of the divided self that separates us from ourselves, from others, from God – and so from our own full potential.

It seems to me impossible to convince people about meditation by mere talk. There is very little point in arguing about it because anyone who meditates begins to meditate because they recognize the truth of it. They *respond* to it. Perhaps they even *remember* it because it is something that seems both to clarify and to *recall* their deepest sense of the meaning of life. This is simply the way reality is structured. If someone wishes to find his or her life he or she *must* first lose it. We know from our ordinary experience that this is the way things are. What we need to find is a practical way which will allow us to apply and to fulfil this knowledge at the deepest level of our being. In this way, at that deepest level, we become one with the very structure of reality. In meditation we enter into harmony with the way things are. And what we learn is this – that we have to enter into the reality of the present moment we have been given before death folds up the past and the future into the eternal. That means that we must learn to die to the ego and the state of egoism that is forever slipping out of the reality of the present by regretting its past or day-dreaming about the future. To meditate is to learn to be present, to be still. *Be still and know that I am God.*[6]

Our ordinary experience is transformed by meditation. With-

5. Jn. 10:10.
6. Ps. 46:10.

out ceasing to be ordinary it becomes deepened by light, truth-
fulness and love. As we begin to meditate our experience, as
it were, validates the risks we have taken in committing ourselves to a way so absurdly, and yet so wonderfully simple. It
does so because meditation brings together the two experiences
of life which most powerfully open our eyes at the deepest level
of perception to the light and structure of reality.

These two experiences are love and death. When we fall
in love our world, both inner and outer, is transformed and
transfigured. The person we love becomes the centre of our
life outside of ourselves. And so we experience the exultant
liberty of spirit which comes from the untying of the self-
centred knot, the ego. All the energy formerly absorbed in
self-consciouness is now freed, enabling us to rejoice in the
person we love, to serve them and to use all the means possible
of deepening and expanding our communion with them. If
there is enough commitment to this communion as a reality that
contains but transcends each individual then the love deepens
beyond the falling in love overture and broadens out through
a lifetime of varied experience of growth and maturing, a
growth and maturity that transforms the whole person and the
whole relationship. This whole person is the person we are
becoming. From birth to death. This whole person is the person
who enters eternal life.

When someone we love dies and when we experience their
dying we return to our own living with a clearer and purer
perception of the true perspective of life simply because we
have participated in the death of one we love – in a death of
a part of ourselves.

And death itself, especially the death of someone we have
loved, teaches us what love teaches us. It reveals to us that the
more deeply we love and enter into communion, so the more
radically we must become detached and non-possessive. To
continue to fall in love we must continue to fall away from the
ego. It is the final and the most demanding of the lessons that
life teaches. It is the meaning of the absolute finality of the
Cross, the single-pointedness of the Cross that yet opens up
into the infinite universe of the Resurrection.

Both in the experience of love and of death we discover the

183

reality of losing self. The wonder of each is to discover that we *can* lose self. In fact, we discover that the very reason for our creation is that we *do* lose self. And this is exactly what our meditation teaches us so well. To lose self, we must stop thinking about ourselves. We must place our centre outside of ourselves, beyond ourselves in another, in *the* Other.

If it is true, as St Benedict tells us, that we must keep death always before our eyes[7] it seems to me that the way of meditation is the supremely natural way to do it. Every time we sit down to meditate we die and so enter more fully into life. Every time we get up and return to the ordinary responsibilities and challenges of life – in family, relationships or at work – we deepen the essential integration of ourselves. It is that integration which is the basis of all the meaning and purpose of life.

Within this vision we see life as preparation for death and we see death as preparation for life. If we are to meet our own death with hope it must be a hope built not on theory or on belief alone but on experience. We must know from experience that *death is an event in life*, an essential part of any life which is a perpetually expanding and self-transcending mystery. It seems to me that only the experience of the continuous death of the ego can lead us into this hope, lead us into an ever-deepening contact with the power of life itself. Only our own death to self-centredness can really persuade us of Death as the connecting link in the chain of perpetual expansion, the way to fullness of life.

The only way to prepare for death is to die day by day. This is a spiritual journey even before it is a religious one. Religion is the sacred expression of the spiritual but if the spiritual experience is lacking then the religious form becomes hollow and superficial and self-important. *Religion does yield high dividends, but only to the person whose resources are within him.*[8]

The interiority of these resources of the eternal reality constitute the spiritual nature of the journey of meditation. But they are interior not introspective. Anyone who meditates in faith

7. *Rule of St Benedict*, ch. 4:47.
8. 1 Tim. 6:6.

184

knows that the journey within takes us out of ourselves. The deeper we penetrate within the more we make contact with others and with the multiplicity and variety of creation. And yet the more wonderfully we see it all in unity – a unity whose centre lies within ourselves. Allow me to read this quotation from St Paul:

> No wonder we do not lose heart. Though our outward humanity is in decay yet day by day we are inwardly renewed. Our troubles are slight and short-lived and their outcome an eternal glory which outweighs them far. Meanwhile our eyes are fixed not on things that are seen but on things that are unseen . . . For what is seen passes away. What is unseen is eternal. We groan indeed because we are enclosed within this earthly frame. We are oppressed because we do not want to have the old body stripped off. Rather our desire is to have the new body put on over it so that our mortal part may be absorbed in life immortal. God himself has shaped us for this very end and as a pledge of it has given us the Spirit. Therefore, we never cease to be confident.[9]

The vision of the *unseen* and the confidence that comes from being absorbed in the *immortal* is what meditation is about. We know with an unshakeable conviction when we die to self that what we stand on is eternal. This is to know that our being may pass through stage to stage of life, through many deaths, but we can never slip out of *being*. God never withdraws the gift he has given and to have given us our being is to have made it immortal. This is the essential preparation we need *in experience* to face our own death without fear, without false consolation, with open minds and open hearts.

Over the years we have been teaching meditation in this tradition we have known people who have started to meditate as they faced death and saw the horizon of their life approaching. Their attitude to death was transformed as they began to die to self day by day, as their preparation for the death of the body. It has been an inspiration and a revelation to us to see their growth in faith and hope as they learned to meditate even

9. 2 Cor. 4:16–5:6.

at this last stage of life. Similarly, it has been an inspiration to see how profoundly the change worked in them and in their attitude to death could influence their family and friends who were making the journey at least part of the way with them.

St Benedict has a chapter in his Rule for monks which he calls *Tools of Good Works* and it is a list of the basic attitudes that the monk has to develop in his life of charity and discipline in order to prepare himself for what St Benedict calls the *divinizing light* of the Kingdom of Heaven. One of these tools or attitudes is to *Keep death always before your eyes*. There is, I think, an extraordinary wisdom in that injunction. Only by keeping death before our eyes can we really learn to be totally childlike in our relation to the ultimate meaning of life. Learning to say the mantra in our daily commitment to meditation is an entry into this childlikeness. For it is this one little word that will root us in the eternal ground of our being and teach us that death is an act of transcendence.

Saying the mantra is learning to die and learning to accept the eternal gift of our being – both in the one act. It is learning that all death is a death to limitation and that if we can die to self we rise to an infinite liberty of love: because love is the creative energy of the universe and also the creative centre of our own being. To find that centre we must go beyond our own self-centredness, we must die to everything that is passing away. As we make this journey and share it with others we enter into the truth that reality is not a final achievement but is a dynamic experience of the passing from self to the other. Only when we have lost our life can we find it.

The way of meditation is a personal way. Dying is a personal journey. No one can meditate for us and no one can die for us. So many barriers and fears come down as a person faces death. So much more freedom is gained to put out our hand to another. And it is the same with meditation.

To follow the way of meditation we need others to travel with us. It is a pilgrimage. The essence of meditation is to be *on the way*. The goal or destination is nothing less than an infinite expansion of being. Pilgrims travel together in faith, supporting and encouraging one another as they go, as they approach at different speeds, and in different ways perhaps, a common goal.

What are the practical conclusions that we can draw from all of this? Conclusions that are relevant to all of us present here – those who care for the dying and for all of us who are on the road that requires that we each face death.

I think they are quite simply these:

– Firstly, we must all prepare for death. Just as we prepare for life by our education so must we prepare for death.

– Secondly, to live fully we must live in relationship with others. We must live our lives with love. To learn to love we must learn to die to self.

– Thirdly, meditation is the perennial wisdom that appears in all ages and all traditions leading us away from egoism and its limitations, into love.

– And finally, meditation is, therefore, well-called in the tradition *the first death*. It is the essential preparation for the second death which is our definitive entry into eternal life.

The View

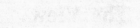

The View

Once upon a time a small boy and his old uncle were out for a walk in their city. It was a large city and had in it all sorts of wonderful modern buildings and wonderful modern people. It was called Secular City and was beautifully situated in a deep valley with spectacular high mountains rising up all around it.

The small boy and his uncle had strayed into an older part of the city, and the boy was very surprised when they came upon a large building in a ruinous condition. This was an altogether unusual sight in the modern city, and the small boy was upset by it. He thought how marvellous the ruins must have looked in their day. Pointing to the ruin, one feature of which seemed to have been a very high tower, he asked his uncle what this ugly eyesore was doing here.

The old uncle sighed; he hated his young nephew to see anything that was ugly. 'Well,' he started, 'I can remember that building well. It was very fine in its day, with a great high tower which reached way up above Secular City. They said that the view from the tower was absolutely stupendous.'

'But how on earth did it become such a ruin?' asked the small boy, looking now with an even greater interest at the noble ruins.

'Well, you see,' the uncle started, 'a rather special group used to live there. They really did a great job for the whole community in rather a strange sort of way. You see in our Secular City we are surrounded by mountains and, as a result, we tend to get rather closed in on ourselves. It's rather difficult to explain, but we tend to think of everything in terms of Secular City. Well, the group that lived there built a large and very high tower – to see the wonderful view; and in some strange way this view of theirs seemed to add a new dimension

191

to the life of the group that made them rather special people in Secular City.'

The boy listened to this explanation with great attention. He wondered how a view could have so changed a group. Turning his innocent face to his uncle, he asked, 'How do you mean – special people? Did the view make them a bit odd?'

'I suppose it did in a way', the uncle replied, trying to recall the group to his mind. 'We could never quite understand why they were so concerned to provide schools and hospitals, orphanages and old people's homes. We just accepted the fact that somehow or other the view was at the back of it all.' He thought very quietly to himself and added: 'Anyone who needed help seemed to become the concern of the group. It all happened a long time ago, and I can't remember too well now; but it seemed that they brought all their talents together and used them wherever there were people in need.'

The uncle had not thought of these things for a long time. It was the dedication of the group that now struck him as the hallmark of their work. He wondered to himself how he had been so lacking in curiosity about the view when the group had been such a creative force in the city.

The little boy now looked really puzzled. 'Well, what happened,' he asked, 'how did it all become a ruin? Did some tyrant come and run them out of town?'

'You remember me telling you about the tower, and how hard it was to climb to the top', the uncle went on. 'Well, it appears that over the years, the staircase that went up to the top got rather old and worn out – I think there was woodworm or maybe dry rot – and the group decided that they would have to rebuild it. And that was when all the trouble started. Some of the group just wanted to repair the staircase, but others said that was no good because the dry rot, or maybe it was wood-worm, would just affect the new wood. Then someone who was really very modern got the idea of pulling down the staircase and putting in an elevator. The trouble with this idea was that they couldn't get the elevator shaft in without pulling down the staircase, and that's when the trouble really started. In the old days, you see, there had always been some of the group either at the top of the stairs looking at the view, or some of them on the way up to encourage the others. I'm not too sure about this, but I think it was rumoured that even before all the discussions started, there weren't quite so many climbing so high up the tower. I think I remember it being said that the group spent a lot of time looking after all their plant and not quite so much time getting up to the view. In any case, they all seemed to agree that the stairs had to be rebuilt. But, when this argument started, they all got so involved in the discussion about the elevator, that they all began to come down to join one of the commissions they set up.'

'What's a commission?' the small boy asked, looking rather puzzled.

The old uncle tried to look very wise. 'A commission,' he faltered, 'was a part of the group set up to examine some particular problem. They usually passed out questionnaires which everybody had to fill in, and these suggested new questions and more questionnaires. I never really understood the process – but I believe it was quite essential.'

The little boy did not seem to be paying much attention to this and, turning his perplexed face to his uncle, he pondered: 'But was anyone trying to keep going up the tower to see the view while those commissions met?' He was only a small boy, but it seemed to him that if the view had been so important in the past it might even inspire the work of the commissions.

'I suppose some were,' replied the old uncle, 'but then they all seemed to get nervous about the foundations.'

'The foundations', replied the small boy, now looking at his old uncle with something like incredulity.

'Yes', went on the uncle. 'You see, after a while the discussions shifted from the question of the elevator or the stairs to another more fundamental matter, namely, would the foundations really support any new structure at all?'

'Well, if they supported the old one, why shouldn't they support the new one?' asked the small boy. 'And, anyway, what about the view? Didn't anyone even want to risk trying to get up to see the view?'

'The problem was,' explained the uncle, 'that the old structure had really become very rickety by this time. The group was finding that the stairs just wouldn't carry them up anymore.

And the foundations, this was quite a problem. But perhaps more serious was another thing. You remember me telling you that in our Secular City we get rather inward looking – strange to say this way of thinking now began to affect the group. In the old days they had brought quite a new dimension to the city, but now somehow or another they became like the rest of the people around them in the city.'

The boy now looked very serious indeed. 'They should have tried to keep contact with that view', he said – his face had become very determined and set.

'I don't think we should be too hard on them,' replied his uncle, 'it was a difficult problem to know how to renew those stairs.' But even as he was saying this, at a deep level he shared his nephew's regret.

'But what happened?' urged the small boy. 'Did the commission ever come up with a solution?' In spite of his black looks of a moment ago, his innocence forced him to believe that there must be a solution.

The old uncle tried to remember. 'I just can't recall', he said. 'There used to be a lot of talk about the group but then people seemed to forget about them.'

It was getting late and they had to be going home, but the small boy wanted to take a closer look at the ruin. They walked over and both looked at one another in surprise. There seemed to be sounds coming from the basement – was someone working at the foundation? But, it was time to go.

'I wonder what the view was really like?' mused the small boy, looking up at the great ruined tower.